# THE DAVID WATKINS STORY

# THE DAVID WATKINS STORY

by David Watkins & Brian Dobbs

PELHAM BOOKS

*First published in Great Britain by*
PELHAM BOOKS LTD
*52 Bedford Square*
*London, W.C.1*
1971



7207 0455 3

*Printed in Great Britain by*
*Northumberland Press Limited*
*Gateshead and bound by*
*the Dorstel Press, Harlow*

# CONTENTS


1 Growing up in Gwent 9

2 Climbing the Ladder 17

3 I Join Wales' Top Club 25

4 How we Beat the All Blacks 33

5 For me my First Cap ... For Wales the Wooden Spoon 42

6 Joint Champions 52

7 Welshmen on the Veldt 59

8 The Triple Crown 67

9 Lions Down Under 77

10 Captain ... With the Skipper on the Touchline 87

11 Dropped 99

12 Mini-Rugby 108

13 I Take the Money 117

14 Gone North ... a Term of Trial 126

15 Wembley Failure 133

16 Reflections 143

Index 149

## ILLUSTRATIONS


*Between pages 16 and 17*

1 THE YOUNG ONES: Captain of the Cwmcelyn Youth team with cups, medals and caps to show.

2 BRINGING HOME THE BACON: I take the 1959 Abertillery Junior Sevens trophy for Cwmcelyn.

3 DISASTER AT STRADEY: Tackled in possession yet again by Aubrey Gale. '... we thought the end of our rugby careers had come.'

4 HAPPIER DAYS: Making a break against Llanelli at Rodney Parade as Newport captain, despite the oncoming John Leleu.

5 THE MAGNIFICENT SEVEN: The 1962 Snelling Cup winners.

6 RUNNING RUGBY: Around the Canadian defences for a Wales Under-23 XV at the Arms Park.

7 JUBILEE TALENT: One of the star-studded fifteens to participate in the South African 75th Anniversary matches in 1964.

*Between pages 48 and 49*

8 THE BIG ONE: One of the better Welsh moments as Robert Morgan evades a 1963 All Black tackle and prepares to pass out to me.

9 SUDDENLY IT ALL CAME GOOD: Through the gap for a try against Ireland in Dublin in 1964, and my best international performance to date.

10 DAY OF DAYS (1): I make one of my few attacking runs for Newport against the 1963 All Blacks.

11 DAY OF DAYS (2): Who says outside halves don't tackle? I prepare to stop Wilson Whineray and Co.

12 DAY OF DAYS (3): The heroes.

13 DAY OF DAYS (4): The move that brought the drop goal as Bob Prosser comes away with John Uzzell, Brian Jones and Dennis Perrott outside him.

14 TRIPLE CROWN CLINCHER: Over for a try against Ireland at Cardiff in 1965, despite a dive by Hewitt of Ireland.

15 MY FINAL INTERNATIONAL: Chaired from the field by the Arms Park crowd after the 1967 match v England.

16 WHAT A WAY TO GO!: The Arms Park scoreboard tells its own story of the fifty-five point thriller.

*Between pages 80 and 81*

17 PIG HUNT: Denzil Williams, myself, Gary Prothero and Brian Price stand triumphant over a New Zealand victim.

18 THE EVILS OF TOBACCO: or The Dangers of Cigarettes for Non Smokers.

19 IN BUSINESS: Moving into top gear against Taranaki.

20 LOWLY SPECTATOR: Picking myself up off the floor as Stan Meads and Hazlett thunder on in the Second Test.

21 ACROSS THE LINE: Even the Christchurch crowd looks pleased as I score a try in the corner in the Third Test.

22 SOLEMN MOMENT: Captain of the Lions in the Final Test and looking as determined as Lochore and Laidlaw.

23 K.O. Aftermath of a difference of opinion with Colin Meads in the Fourth Test.

*Between pages 112 and 113*

24 CONGRATULATIONS AND JUBILATIONS: A Union send-off for the new League player.

25 HAPPY BAPTISM: Haring off for Salford and on the way to my first try in rugby league.

26 AIMING FOR WEMBLEY: In full flight for the Warrington defence in the Rugby League Cup semi-final at Wigan.

27 DRESSING ROOM EMOTION: Mr Snape, myself and the Salford team celebrate the win over Warrington and drink a toast to a victory at Wembley.

28 THEY ALSO SERVE ...: Colin Dixon and Charlie Bott in the thick of the Wembley action.

The authors and publishers wish to thank the following sources for the photographs used in the plates. *Western Mail and South Wales Echo*: 3, 4, 5, 6, 12. *Sport and General*: 8. *South Wales Argus*: 9, 10, 11, 13, 15, 16. *Evening Post, Wellington*: 18, 19, 20. *V. C. Browne, Christchurch*: 21. *Syndication International*: 26. *John Mountfield*: 27. *Topix*: 28.

# 1. GROWING UP IN GWENT

That I spent the first eighteen years of my life at 6 Club Row, Blaina in Monmouthshire might not mean very much to a non-Welsh reader. Let me explain that Blaina is a small village firmly in the tradition of the Welsh mining valleys. My father and his father before him were miners. My grandfather spent 62 years underground, my father has been a miner for 36 years and there was a time when I wanted to go down the pit myself.

I mention this coal background as only those who have lived in a mining community can understand how closely-knit we were. The people in Blaina have somehow shared in what success I've had in sport and I was surrounded by goodwill and local best wishes from the first tentative steps I took towards the top of a sporting ladder higher than I could ever have anticipated.

The outsider would be wrong if he thought that my growing up in such a rugby stronghold meant that I was hugging a rugby ball in my cradle. The only rugby player in my family history was my mother's father, Sem Bridgeman. He played on the wing for Newbridge in the twenties, but those were the days when Welsh rugby was in the international doldrums. Ironically, when he'd retired from playing he became absorbed in watching, not rugby, but soccer, and it was this influence as much as anything else which rubbed off on me.

The children of Blaina were sports mad and from my

earliest days so was I. Television had not spread across the valleys then, and every evening and Saturday morning, rain or shine, we would be out in the street, or in the local park, playing and playing for hours. If ever I allowed myself a Walter Mitty sporting dream, it would have been imagining myself as a professional soccer player. Possibly there were occasions when I'd hear a radio commentary on a rugby international and spend ten minutes running about pretending I was Tony O'Reilly, but I soon forgot it. Really rugby was a closed book to me.

Soccer was different. It was the ruling passion of my life. At Christmas time my two brothers and I would be asking for kit. Money wasn't easily come by but every December 25th, there would be a football or new boots or a cricket bat, or stumps. We lacked for nothing in the way of sports equipment, and we were given parental encouragement to play whenever and whatever we chose.

My first pair of football boots arrived when I was six. No pair of boots in football history was cherished more. I wore them to play, I wore them to walk around the house —given the chance I'd have worn them to bed. I can even remember creating a fuss because I wasn't allowed to wear them with my best Sunday suit to go on the bus to my grandmother's in Abertillery for Sunday tea. I was so excited by football kit that I was reluctant to take it off.

For children, we were pretty well organised. Our first real venture was a Club Row football team. The only field we had available was triangular. Undeterred, we marked out a suitable pitch. There were only coats for goalposts and to square the field off we had to incorporate a road running through the middle of the playing area. With the enthusiasm of youth, I would walk to the other end of Blaina just for buckets of sawdust to mark out the lines for a local derby against a team from the neighbouring pre-fabs. Club Row v Pre-fabs—it meant as much as a Wembley cup final.

The allocation of pocket money was no problem. All I wanted from my mother was enough money to go with my grandfather to a soccer match. One Saturday we would meet up at the local bus-stop to go to see Newport County, and the next at the station to go on the special train to Cardiff City.

My cherished memories and sporting inspirations did not come from seeing Cliff Morgan at the Arms Park score dazzling 50 yard tries or Malcolm Thomas sidestepping through the centre at Rodney Parade—I would hardly have known who they were. My hero-worship was reserved for Ray Wilcox, the Newport County centre-half and captain battling in desperate defence in a third round F.A. Cup match at home to the mighty Arsenal; or for Gerry Hitchens, pounding down the middle of Ninian Park, with the rumbustious Trevor Ford alongside him. Cardiff, at that time, were in the First Division and one could see all the great soccer players of the day, and savour the atmosphere of 40 and 50,000 people roaring on the Bluebirds. How could rugby have compared with this?

I did see one rugby match, and that was a Welsh Trial. A schoolteacher from Nantyglo, Graham Powell, the Ebbw Vale centre, was the first man from our valley for a long time to be in with a chance of a Welsh cap, and enough of the local enthusiasm rubbed off on me for me to go with some friends to Cardiff Arms Park to see the first trial. With perhaps 10,000 others scattered on the vast terraces of the Arms Park in the pouring rain, we watched not the game, but Graham Powell in the centre. All ignorance and Watkins impudence, I came away soaking wet and saying 'Yes, of course Graham Powell should play for Wales.' No other spark was kindled in me. Nothing in the event made me want to forsake Ninian Park or

Somerton Park to watch rugby regularly.

There was worse to come. At the age of eleven, I left the West Side Junior School where there had been no organised sport and we could play casual schoolyard soccer to our hearts' content, and went to Glanyrafon Secondary Modern School. Like most valley secondary schools, this was a rugby school. There was no soccer team, and the sports master was Russell Cooper. We didn't know it then but he had been a fine back row forward, playing for the London Welsh, had had many a duel with Cliff Morgan and the other fly-halves of the day, and was unlucky never to be capped.

My first initiation to rugby, which could have been advanced trigonometry for all I knew about it, was essentially brutal. The new boys were divided into teams for the Under Thirteen trials. I was small but very fast for my age. Running everywhere at full speed was a compulsion. 'Young Watkins—wing three-quarter.' There were no sophisticated facilities for schools then and this match was played in the school yard. It was either there, or on the uneven surface of a coal tip, so this was the lesser of two evils.

The first five minutes I watched in interested idleness out on the wing. Then, by some miracle, the ball reached me. Clutching it under my arm I careered off down the side-line. My moment of glory was brief. Mercilessly I was charged into touch by a taller, heavier boy and my head banged into an iron railing. I saw stars and was helped away to have a deep cut attended to.

That did it. I swore I'd never play rugby again. Rugby was supposed to be compulsory but nothing was going to force me to play so barbaric a sport. 'You will play rugby!' 'No, I won't!' 'All right then, you'll have to do mathematics while the others play rugby.' 'All right, suits me.'

For some time, I did this. The other boys took their

kit and went out into the sunshine to play, and their shouts filtered through the window to me, sitting in a deserted classroom struggling with logarithms. Perhaps this was a subtle form of psychological warfare, for I soon began to regret the haste with which I'd made up my mind.

There were other pressures. To be in the school's first XV carried great prestige. The annual team photographs were hung on the wall and to appear in one of those certainly appealed. The girls in the school looked more warmly on the he-men of the rugby team than on the academics. Rugby was the perennial topic of conversation among the boys and their enthusiasm began to get me involved. Schoolboys can be just like sheep and one doesn't question values very much at the age of thirteen or fourteen. Perhaps I didn't have the moral courage to be determinedly different, so I gave in.

Soon I was playing regularly, now at scrum-half. Because I was naturally fast and elusive, I had some measure of success. I played my first game for the school against Gelli Grug Secondary Modern, and probably purely due to my ignorance of the arts of rugby football, I slanted away on the open-side of a scrum and ran sixty yards for a try. There was enjoyment to be had from this game, after all.

Russell Cooper continued to encourage and foster my new interest. Before long, my zeal for soccer had been transferred. I threw myself into rugby as enthusiastically as I had into soccer before. Suddenly, the game got into the blood—I lived for rugby football.

Sundays would entail a visit to Blaina's rugby ground, Cwmcelyn Park. We would meet there at 10 o'clock in the morning, play non-stop rugby in knock-out competitions, triangular tournaments, marathon matches, the lot. Barely dragging one foot after the other, I would limp home at

7 o'clock in the evening to announce proudly that we'd won 840 points to 614 and I'd scored 17 tries. It was survival of the fittest. One legacy of those days may be the physical pleasure I still get from training, almost as much as from playing, though it might be the compulsive running of a schoolboy who never grew up.

Naturally, the Club Row soccer team was disbanded. My mother's sitting room became the official dressing room of the Club Row Rugby XV. Known locally as the Rainbow team, we must have presented a comical sight. Fifteen players, or as near as we could get to fifteen, playing in positions which no one knew much about, and the confusion absolute with every player in a different coloured jersey. It took quite a few Christmases to rationalise the kit situation.

Joy of joys, we were loaned a field about 70 yards by 50 at the back of the house, and to us, clattering through the house and up the steps to trot out on to the grass, it was Wales running out at Twickenham to smash England. My mother, less romantically, was left with 15 multi-coloured jerseys to wash out with no more than a rubbing board to help her.

The new game took me over absolutely, and the new enthusiasm reached some absurd lengths. When Geoff Whitson, the Newport back-row forward married a Blaina girl at a local chapel, I and a school friend of mine Bryn Howells, who was rugby crazy, picked up the unlikely news that the whole Welsh team would be attending. We were outside the chapel at 8 o'clock in the morning drizzle, patiently waiting to see them. All we actually saw hours later was Geoff Whitson going in a bachelor and coming out a married man, but even that made our day.

Choosing school prizes was easy. You were allowed to select your own book title and I can remember asking for, and receiving, Haydn Tanner's book on rugby and, to complete the thrill, being presented with it on speech day by Cliff Morgan, the principal guest speaker.

All my involvement and time was not, however, matched by progress in schools representative rugby. I began to hear critics saying that I was far too small to play rugby. Although I was short, I was fairly sturdy and I resented the prejudice. Size is irrelevant in senior rugby, because one has by then had to prove one's ability to get there at all, but it can hamper one's progress in junior grades considerably.

My first bitter disappointment came when I was picked as the reserve scrum-half for the Abertillery and Blaina Schools v the Rhymney Valley Schools. This was played on a home and away basis. I turned up for the first leg to find that the first choice scrum-half was injured and could not play. Before I had recovered from the excitement of hearing this, the selection committee had eyed my lack of inches, decided I was too small to play rugby and official reserve or not, I was not allowed to play.

Russell Cooper was a member of the committee, but he was absent on the day. I suspect that he created such a rumpus in the next meeting at my treatment that the rest of the selectors gave in. I played in the return as first choice, more, I am sure, to mollify him and me than for my innate ability as a scrum-half. We lost the game but apparently I'd showed some promise. My outside-half, incidentally, was Arthur Lewis who won his first Welsh cap against France at the end of the 1969-70 season as a centre.

Schools rugby did not bring me a great deal of rugby fortune. I was in the school team which reached the final of the Monmouthshire Schools knock-out cup at Blaina Park but we lost 19-6. At that match, the schools selectors found a temporary ally in my mother.

She had never seen a rugby game before and my father took her to see me in the final. After a few minutes of the game, I made a run to be collared by a wing-forward and disappeared under a pile of players rucking furiously. She was horrified. 'Jack, quick,' she said to my father, 'get our David off there before he gets hurt.' He fortunately was made of sterner stuff and abandoned her on the touchline in her agitation, to watch uninterrupted. She soon got over it, of course, and has since become as enthusiastic a spectator as any. With my younger brothers Brian and Martin playing local rugby as well, she's had to be.

At fifteen, I left school to start work in an apprentice scheme for foremen and managers at an Ebbw Vale steel works. That meant the end of the days when rugby was an automatic part of one's weekly timetable. If I wanted to continue playing, I had to find a team for myself.

The Young Ones: Captain of the Cwmcelyn Youth team with cups, medals and caps to show.

Bringing Home the Bacon: I take the 1959 Abertillery Junior Sevens trophy for Cwmcelyn.

Disaster at Stradey: Tackled in possession yet again by Aubrey Gale.
'. . . we thought the end of our rugby careers had come.'

HAPPIER DAYS: Making a break against Llanelli at Rodney Parade as Newport captain, despite the oncoming John Leleu.

THE MAGNIFICENT SEVEN: The 1962 Snelling Cup winners. *Back Row* Byron Thomas, Brian Price, Glyn Davidge, Brian Jones. *Front* Bob Prosser, Bryn Meredith and a nervous D.W.

Running Rugby: Around the Canadian defences for a Wales Under-23 XV at the Arms Park.

Jubilee Talent: One of the star-studded fifteens to participate in the South African 75th Anniversary matches in 1964. *Back Row* Ellwood (Aus), du Preez (SA), A. Malan (SA), Clarke (NZ), Marais (SA). *Middle Row* Briscoe (NZ) Botha, Hopwood, van Wyck, Myburgh, Truter (all SA). *Front Row* S. F. Kingsley (SARU), Flynn (Ire), G. Malan (SA) *capt*, D.W. (Wales), Hughes (Aus).

# 2. CLIMBING THE LADDER

I had watched the local Cwmcelyn Youth Club rugby team a number of times. They had been getting a fair amount of local press attention and had produced some fine players for senior rugby. I went along and I asked if I could join.

I was no Welsh schoolboy star groomed for higher things and raw as I was, there was no good reason for them to welcome me with open arms. The youth age limits were very strictly applied and by a happy coincidence, the team's outstanding outside-half, Evan Davies, had had to drop out at the end of the previous season. The club officials looked dubiously at my diminutive stature so perhaps I had sufficiently wistful an expression on my face for them to take pity on me. Reluctantly they admitted that they were without an outside-half, so I could have the place temporarily to see what I could make of it. I was issued with a black jersey with a number 6 on the back for this was before the numbering changed and 10 became the standard number for a fly-half. I had played in the position occasionally at school and Russell Cooper had said that this would be my natural position if I ever made it in senior rugby.

My speed proved my biggest asset. I fitted in to my new team and they seemed to fit in with me. I kept the place and we began to win matches. The team was exceptionally well run by two dedicated officials, Rowland Hill and

Rumsey James, and the more matches we won, the more attention we began to get. We might draw 300 or 400 people along to see us, a large crowd for a youth game. Even at this level, playing to win began to matter more and more. I had always been competitive by nature and I thrived on the atmosphere of playing in a winning team. The more we won, the more the club progressed. A collection from the crowd meant that we no longer had to pay 2s each towards the cost of the bus for away matches. The Blaina rugby club, seeing the team as a potential breeding ground for senior players, donated a set of jerseys. We got more and more press attention, and we barely lost a game all season.

I received individual notices too. I found I could use my speed and my elusiveness to beat opposing players. I made the sort of runs that could have had me shot in senior rugby—running horizontally across the field and doubling back, going backwards before going forwards, and yet somehow the unorthodox worked. I could indulge all my natural attacking instincts. We entered a Cwmcelyn side for the Joseph Falkman Sevens trophy, a cup for junior club sides. Against teams composed mostly of senior players, our side, young, nippy and cheeky walked away with it. When we went on to win the Monmouthshire youth cup, I can remember being carried shoulder high through the main street of Blaina preceded by the local brass band. We won the trophy again for the following three years. In fact, I never played on a losing sevens side for Cwmcelyn, and we pocketed every trophy going.

The Monmouthshire youth selectors were not particularly impressed. 'Watkins—too small for representative youth rugby.' I had to wait until the following season when I became captain of the team before they were prepared to try me. I don't think I'd grown any, so I was just happy they'd changed their minds

My Monmouthshire partner was to be Alan Lewis, a scrum-half from Pontypool Youth. Little did either of us realise then that ours would later become a partnership for Wales and for the British Lions. Alan was a great asset to me at this stage. He had a long accurate service which helped to get me out beyond the reach of the contemporary scourge of outside-halves, the fast breaking wing-forward. My outside break was my best, and Alan could feed this marvellously. It is as much due to him as to anyone that the post brought the most important communication I'd ever received.

Printed in red, in letters that seemed a foot high, on a postcard headed Welsh Youth Rugby Union, it was an invitation to play in the Welsh Youth trial at Bridgend. 'Please let me know by return post whether you are able to play.' I couldn't fill it in fast enough. I even wondered whether I should deliver my reply personally to West Wales in case it got lost in the post. It was way beyond any dream I'd ever had. Suddenly to be on the verge of international honours, the very thought made me tremble. Nervous though I was, the trial itself went well for me. They were picking the team which was to play against the Welsh Secondary Schools at Stradey Park directly after the match. We could stay in the clubhouse, if we liked to wait to hear the team, if we wanted to. Naturally, we stayed. The selectors closeted themselves in a committee room, and stayed there for two hours.

It was like being on the outside of a jury room. I paced up and down. I reviewed the game in my mind a hundred times. Had I kicked enough? Had I kicked too much? Had I done enough covering? Had I held the ball too long? My father kept saying, 'You'll be all right, you did enough to get in,' but I knew he was bound to be biased. Eventually the chairman of the youth selectors came out with a list in his hand.

There was a deathly silence as he said, 'Here is the team to play against the Welsh Secondary Schools at Stradey Park on 27th February, 1960.' From that moment to this, I've had fellow feeling for parliamentary candidates as the returning officer goes through a long preamble before giving the result of an election. 'Full-Back ... Wing ... Centres ... Wing ... Outside-half ... It seemed an hour passed between 'Full-Back ...' and 'Outside-half ...' and another hour between 'Outside-half...' and '... David Watkins!' Relief! Jubilation! Thrilled to bits! The official card came next day but I still went out to buy the *Western Mail* and the South Wales *Football Echo* on the Saturday, partly to make sure and partly for the sheer joy of seeing my name in print.

The game at Stradey Park we lost 11-6. My opposite number was Beverley Davies who I met again later in senior Welsh trials. That we lost, I freely confess, meant much less to me than that I thought I'd played well. I made some attacking runs, had kicked accurately and, although it wasn't particularly expected of young fly-halves, I'd used my speed to cover tackle as much as possible. This wasn't the influence of a coach, just something I developed naturally, for I've always been an instinctive sort of player.

My first indication that instinct alone cannot make a rugby footballer came from one of the selectors after the game. He was Cliff Jones, one of the greatest ever Welsh fly-halves who had spearheaded Wales to victory over the All Blacks in 1936. Naturally, his words were to be treated as gospel. If he'd told me I could improve my game by jumping in the Taff, I'd have done so. He was very encouraging about my performance but explained kindly that I was too right-footed as a kicker. Work on the left foot as well was his advice.

That was enough for me. Next morning saw me at the foot of a Blaina coal-tip, with a boot on my left foot and a sock on the right. This was the only place I could get kicking practice without the tedium of fetching the ball every time. I kicked it up the incline and twenty seconds later the ball would run back down to me to be gathered and kicked on the turn back up the slope. If I had a lapse of concentration, the impact of a heavy wet ball encrusted with coal dust on a stockinged right foot was a painful reminder. Months of this and I began to kick as well with the left foot as with the right.

The match reports from Stradey Park were kind, and one commentator was moved to suggest that I might be another Cliff Morgan on the horizon. Considered objectively, this might have been thought an unfair tag to put on so young a player. I was more naïve then and it made me feel ten feet tall. Since then, I've kept every cutting good or bad. Press criticism is a factor a young player has to learn to live with, and I found that praise at that stage merely fed my ambitions to get on in the game.

I was retained in the Welsh Youth side for the next match—against France at Tulle. Nothing could have caused me more excitement. I had never been abroad before, and the preparations caused as much frenzied activity in the family as if I'd been leaving on a Polar expedition. There was someone to volunteer to fetch my passport, someone to organise inoculations, someone to contribute to pocket money; and telegrams, cards and letters arriving to wish me well. If necessary, I swear all Blaina would have got me on that plane.

Any apprehension I had about my first flight was swallowed by the knowledge that at the end of it, I'd be playing for Wales in a foreign country in a red jersey with three feathers on it. For that, I'd have swum to France. Enthusiasm was not even tempered by the knowledge that conditions would be of the kind we'd never come across before and that we had a formidable French team to contend with. How formidable none of us realised as our coach sped from Bordeaux through the French countryside to Tulle.

Our team, with Gary Prothero as captain at No. 8, was a talented Welsh youth side, but the French side with Gachassin at fly-half was faster than any side we'd ever met. With the unique natural running and passing talents that the French always seem to develop, they threw the ball about with abandon. The forwards seemed as fast as the backs, and with the temperature soaring up to the 80s, a ground so hard there were boys with sandbuckets to make artificial tees for goalkicking, and a noisy French crowd of 5,000 roaring their team on, we were overrun.

My strongest memory of the game is the number of times I had to drop out after a French score. It was a long practice session for they ran up 36 points. We failed to reply. Someone suggested that we went home and pretended that the wrong score had been transmitted in error and that it was really 3-6, but we agreed that we'd never get away with it.

It wasn't quite the humiliation it sounded and we came away with a surprising amount of praise from the French press, both as individuals and as a team, for sticking it out to the bitter end and still trying, long after it became obvious that we were on a hiding to nothing. I arrived back in Blaina with an armful of French cuttings and wandered around asking likely people to translate.

'Can you tell me, please, what it says after *Le Petit Watkins*...?'

The Youth Selectors evidently agreed that there was no need to wield an axe and I retained my place for the last international of the season against a strong Midlands Colts XV, which was really a misnomer for England. We won 6-3 and then I had an unexpected end of season bonus. The youth age limit was lifted by a year, and I qualified for one more youth season. For good measure, youth players were also to be permitted a maximum of four senior games in the next season.

Pontypool R.F.C. were the first to take advantage of this. Their regular outside-half, Benny Jones, was injured. Would I play against Pontypridd for them? Of course I would! Pontypool—the reigning Welsh champions! No bother at all! Theirs was an excellent team—Ray Cheney at full back, Fenton Coles on the wing, Colin Evans at scrum-half, and Ray Prosser in the pack. Playing at outside-half with colleagues like that—it didn't seem possible.

The game, for which I was ready about four hours too early, went well for me. A Youth outside-half, faced with a wing-forward like Ken Leonard of Pontypridd, is naturally vulnerable. In a less experienced side than Pontypool, I could have finished with a persecution complex after 80 minutes, but inexperience can also work in your favour. With so many attacking players in the Pontypool side, Pontypridd could not afford to worry too much about the new boy. Colin Evans gave me the ball only when I was in a position to use it properly, so Ken Leonard was left to chase me around as I put in some attacking runs. We lost but I went home happy.

I also guested that year for Blaina, scoring 3 tries at centre, for Ebbw Vale against Swansea and for Abertillery in the Bridgend Sevens. That, and the end of my Youth football after the season's three Youth internationals provoked speculation. Where would Watkins go? To be honest, I had little idea myself and I tried to gather advice to help me make up my mind. If you don't know the way ask a policeman, so I asked the local policeman.

He was no ordinary copper. He was Inspector R. T.

Evans, one of the most formidable Welsh back row forwards of all time. I never saw him play for Newport or for Wales, but his ruthless tackling of opposing backs and three-quarters is still legendary in Welsh Rugby circles. He was a man to be listened to.

'Write to Newport and ask for a trial,' he said 'they'll look after you.' My immediate reaction was that even a letter to such a top club would be a waste of time. He persuaded me that I would be better off in a top club even playing in the United side than taking my chances in one of the valley teams. Even remembering counsels from the Blaina Chairman that a season or two with Blaina before venturing into big-time rugby would be more to my advantage, I made up my mind. I sat down and wrote to Newport.

# 3. I JOIN WALES' TOP CLUB

Almost by return, I had a letter inviting me to play for the Black and Amber side in the first trial. The system operated was for two sides of new players to play in the first trial on a Saturday, and the best fifteen to be selected for the following Wednesday to play for the Colours against the Black and Ambers which became the previous season's first team. With all sorts of doubts and half-suppressed hopes running through my mind, I swayed from side to side in a bus down the valley to Newport.

Without false modesty, I can say I had no suspicions at all that I might myself be valuable to a club of Newport's standing. I walked from the bus station towards the ground with a kit bag in one hand and my cap metaphorically in the other. Waiting for me on the bridge across the river was Bill Everson, the football secretary. He took me to the Rodney Parade ground and was kindness itself. In later years, he acted almost as a second father to me and was such a superb administrator that Newport almost ran as Bill Everson R.F.C. That an official of some standing should take the trouble to meet a boy down from the valleys for a trial, I never questioned. In my naïvety, I never questioned either that I was to be partnered in the trial by Billy Watkins, Newport's regular scrum-half and a Welsh international. As a rule, an established Newport player would never play in a first trial. Billy and I hit it off in the game, where he gave me the sort of service and protection that helped me conquer my nerves. After the match, I was invited to come back and play for the Colours on the Wednesday.

In the second trial, I had a good first half, and without even then seeing the implications, was told to exchange jerseys with Geoff Davies, the first choice fly-half. Of the second half, I can remember nothing. I was excited certainly but I didn't allow myself to think of anything beyond trying to avoid dropping the ball or giving away a try.

The following evening, I had an unexpected visitor from the police station. Inspector Evans was on the doorstep. 'You'll be playing for Newport against Penarth in the opening match of the season.' 'You must be joking!' 'No, the selectors met this evening and you'll get an official card in the morning.' It was true.

It was only as I walked over Newport Bridge for the third time in eight days that the full implications hit me. Spectators were already walking towards the ground. I was going to put a black and amber shirt on and play for Newport. By the time I'd reached the dressing room and looked around in a daze, it seemed more and more like a wishful daydream. The rest of the team were changing and I felt like a spectator who'd taken a wrong turning and wandered into the dressing room. Brian Jones, Billy Watkins, Glyn Davidge, Geoff Whitson, Brian Cresswell, Ian Ford, Brian Price, Bryn Meredith, all Welsh internationals—these were the people you read about, not played with. They must have known how I felt for they made every effort to make me feel at home.

Brian Jones came over and reassured me. 'You've nothing to worry about, just play your natural game.' Before the game, Bryn Meredith gave his team talk as captain. He welcomed me to the team and told the other players that here was a boy in his first venture into big football whom he wanted looked after. It was all very flattering, little Dai with fourteen father figures. R. T. Evans proved to be right and, with no disrespect to any other club, I do not think that I could have had the same sort of treatment elsewhere. The sheer presence of a line-out jumper like Brian Price, or the perfection of a back-row forward like Glyn Davidge, gave one greater things to play for.

Looking back now ten years on, I still look on that first season with Newport as a honeymoon period. Securicor couldn't have done a better job of protection for me than that Newport side. When trouble was in the offing, I didn't get the ball. When I did, it was because a break was possible. That season, I was able to run with the ball, carve out openings, score tries and indulge all my attacking instincts. At the end of my first season we were unofficial Welsh Champions. I remember that first game against Penarth vividly. Early on, I broke away around the Penarth back-row and down the touchline for 60 yards before putting Dennis Perrott into the corner. After that, I sensed the Rodney Parade crowd was behind me and midway through the second half, I had a golden opportunity to crown the display.

A Penarth forward came out of their 25 with the ball held in front of him. I moved in to tackle and he proferred it to me in a half-hearted dummy. Instinctively I snatched it out of his hands, sidestepped him, sidestepped two other Penarth players and touched down under the posts. The crowd were delirious and the headlines next day were full of 'Newport's new star'. 'Roy Burnett's successor', 'Watkins—the new Cliff Morgan.'

Up to this point, my story has had a Roy of the Rovers boys' comic unreality about it. Valley boy makes good. Cwmcelyn to Welsh Youth to playing for Newport. Season of seasons. This is exactly how it was. I got the ball, I ran, I beat my man—surely this was what rugby was all about.

I was in for some rude awakenings.

The first came from Bryn Meredith. Bryn, who earned more Welsh caps than any other forward, had been in the game a good deal longer than I had. He soon brought me back to earth. I played my first away fixture for Newport at Leicester. Playing for a first-class club meant the sort of treatment that V.I.P.s get. We were entertained to lunch in the restaurant at Newport Station, given a reserved compartment to Leicester and chauffeured to a hotel by private coach for a rest before the game. Kit was supplied and looked after by a baggage man. All one had to do was to turn up.

We lost the game 11-6 but I had a particularly good match. As I remember, I scored the two tries and brought off two saving tackles on Leicester players twice my size. Full of immature enthusiasm, I looked forward to the reports, and must have had a satisfied smirk on my face.

Bryn's first remark was a jolt.

'I don't see what you've got to be so pleased about—we lost.' I couldn't understand why he was getting at me.

'What's the good of you playing well if the team go and lose? Newport the club is more important than David Watkins.'

He had plenty to say on the subject of press reports. Don't bother to read them was his view. Supposing your centre is hiding an injury and doesn't want the ball. You kick all afternoon which is the right thing to do, and next morning's paper will crucify you for obsessive kicking without knowing the truth. You've played well in context but you won't get any credit for it. It was good advice, for only later, when I was captain of the side, did I come to realise that the only real appreciation worth having was the respect of your fellow players. A wing might collar the headlines for scoring tries but the players' respect was probably reserved for the centre who was unobtrusively laying on the scoring passes. Whatever the press says, whatever the public thinks, if you're well thought of by the players you're playing with and against, that means everything. Mind you, I went on collecting my cuttings.

Two major influences on my rugby emerged—Peter Rees and Brian Jones. The two of them were in every way players' players. They lived rugby and, more important, they knew rugby. Brian had perhaps lost a yard of his pace since his international days but what he didn't know about rugby wouldn't cover a match ticket. As a talker on the game, or as a tactical thinker, he was almost unique. Brian and Peter's loyalty to Newport was absolute. If you cut either of them, their blood would come out black and amber. They had also learned to curb their own play, in the centre and on the wing, if the interests of Newport demanded it.

They have since become personal friends quite outside rugby and if they have something to say about the game, I listen. Unfortunately, it wasn't always so. 'Play to the team and the situation,' they'd say. 'O.K.' I'd say, and go my own sweet way. Growing up, in rugby, as in life, can be a long painful process. One of my obsessions was having to beat the opposing wing-forward myself. If I didn't get round him with the ball in my hands and leave him on the deck, it was some sort of personal failure. The tougher and rougher the wing-forward, the more it meant to me to beat him. You can see a parallel in soccer, where Georgie Best in his early days, with three Manchester United forwards screaming for the ball in front of an empty net, would be totally absorbed not in the situation, but in trying to make the full-back look a fool. I knew just how Georgie was feeling.

For me, Newport v Bridgend and Newport v Neath meant Watkins v Leighton Davies and Watkins v Allan Dix. They, like any wing-forward worth his salt, would rile me. For the first ten minutes they'd give me the treatment, tell me I was chicken; little Watkins you're soft. I didn't have the discretion to play to the situation. It became a personal vendetta. Without the inner discipline to concentrate on trying to read the game, I tried to answer force with force. Me, ten stone nothing and five foot six and trying to knock a big man about. The result was invariably that I'd finish on the floor under them and the ball and Newport's attack would die with me.

'B.J.' and Peter would be furious. A player of my ability had no need to tangle like that. Of course they'll ridicule you, of course they'll be happy if you let yourself be affected, you're playing into their hands.

I could accept their arguments intellectually because they made sense. And yet the next time Leighton or Allan came at me, something inside me would snap and off we'd go on a private duel again and Newport would lose because of it. Young, hot headed, knew it all.

A few years later, we took Bridgend's ground record because I disciplined myself. Leighton Davies would come towards me and I'd get rid of the ball before he could touch me. By the time he was up out of the scrum I'd passed or I'd kicked. The result was that he was the one who got riled and he went off his game.

Playing for Newport not for Watkins was a hard learned lesson. Few outsiders ever realise the competitive nature of Welsh club rugby. A Newport match against Neath or Bridgend or Llanelli or, of course, against Cardiff, is a mini-international. Even regular spectators cannot know the tension and the will to win engendered in the dressing room. There is no difference in coming out to play against Cardiff than in playing for Wales against England. Victory means so much. Welsh rugby at this level isn't a matter of a Saturday hobby, it's something you're living with constantly. I would have it no other way.

Winning rugby at this level is only possible for the side which plans, thinks and disciplines itself to come out on top. Brian and Peter and I would spend hours in a hotel after a game, analysing, dissecting, discussing and arguing.

In 1964 when I became captain of Newport, which I remained until I turned professional, it was the way I had to think. I was, incidentally, the youngest Newport captain since Jack Morley, the famous Newport, Wales and British Lion wing three-quarter of the twenties. Winning rugby, efficient rugby, percentage rugby, that's what brings in the crowds. When Newport carry off the Welsh club championship the club shows a profit. I could go out against Blackheath or Harlequins, and throw the ball about. Running rugby with all the frills, in the William Webb Ellis tradition, is always possible against English sides. Against Blackheath, one might make a dozen breaks and be looking round for opponents to beat before going over the tryline. Against Neath you'd make one if you were lucky, and that had to be the match-winner.

In Wales, guards had to be up not only against the big boys but against all the valley clubs. For Abertillery, or Newbridge or Ebbw Vale, to beat Newport or Cardiff is a highpoint of their season. I can remember losing to Abertillery 8-6 on a Boxing Day at Rodney Parade for the first time for about 15 years. I was given a lift home on the Abertillery team bus and we pulled up en route at a café for everyone to be bought a meal in honour of the victory over Newport. In the jubilation, you'd have sworn Abertillery had won the Triple Crown.

Ebbw Vale brings back memories too. For two years running we went there and played pretty pretty football. Ebbw Vale lay back, waited for mistakes and booted the ball ruthlessly downfield. Two years running they won. When I took the team there as captain, we played it tight.

Ten minutes from the end it was still 3-3 and we won 25-3. Grumbles all round. Newport didn't come up here to play football at all. I said 'Aye, we came up here too many times playing football and losing. If you want us to run the ball, you must run the ball. Otherwise we can play as hard and as tight as you can—and win.'

The tension of four matches a season against Cardiff never troubled me. In fact, I seemed to reserve some of my best games for Cardiff. One game under floodlights stands out, Brian Jones was at full-back deputising for John Anthony, who was injured. Brian had great difficulty in fielding the ball when it went high above the lights, and every time he missed or dropped it I was in position to pick it up or tackle or kick. Roy Morgan, the Cardiff No. 8 was even diving over the line for a try on one occasion when I snatched the ball out of his hands and made a 25 yard run up the field. I didn't score, I didn't make a scoring break but I know it was one of my best ever games for Newport.

That is the difference. Fresh from Cwmcelyn, a great game was when you scored three tries, not when you helped others to win the game for your team. Now I can see it. If it is necessary to kick for 80 minutes to win the game, you must kick for 80 minutes. The responsibility of being captain did a lot for me in this way. I learned not to take too much on myself. There are fourteen other men in the side, you have to think of them.

Learning the finer arts of rugby as a team game and learning to read a game is obviously a gradual process. If there was any one event to which I could pin my own transformation from an enthusiastic youth to a disciplined player, it was when we beat the All Blacks in 1963. In the words of B.J. that was when little Dai became a man. The whole victory meant so much to me, to Newport and to Wales, it is worth recounting in detail.

# 4. HOW WE BEAT THE ALL BLACKS

Wednesday, October 30th, 1963, was a day of days. It was then, and looking back it is probably even more so now. Not only were we the only club or international side to beat the All Blacks on that tour, but at the time of writing nearly eight years later, we still remain the last club side to do so. The importance of the occasion has grown rather than dimmed over the years.

For Newport, the game didn't start at 3 p.m. on that Wednesday. As soon as the New Zealanders arrived for their tour, we had our spies out assessing the quality of the opposition. They played their first match of the tour against Oxford University at Oxford winning impressively 19-3, and then crushed Southern Counties at Brighton 32-3. In attendance at Oxford was a Newport contingent including Brian 'Ben' Price, then Newport captain, Brian Jones and Ian McJennett, who was acting as coach with Bryn Meredith.

Some critics have tried to take the edge off the Newport victory by saying that meeting them in the third match of the tour gave us an advantage. In one way it did, but 19-3 and 32-3 does not suggest a side taking time to settle down. Also meeting them so early ourselves, did not give us much chance to weigh up all *their* tactics, particularly when they made thirteen changes for the second game.

The spies came back with some definite conclusions. The adversaries were formidable but not unbeatable. They had adopted a line-out ploy from the French, of a forward peeling off the end of the line and running with the ball to draw the defence. On one side of the field, Nathan would do this and Whineray would do it on the other—predictable but effective. It meant that we were then tempted to pull a back-row forward out of the line to cover him. We would be weak at the back of the line-out and they could drive through there instead.

Brian, Ian and 'Ben' Price came up with a counter. This was before the ten yards offside law was introduced and the three-quarters were allowed to lie up on the advantage line. Consequently, when Nathan or Whineray came away, it was the job of Brian Jones or Dick Uzzell in the centre to tackle them. This meant a ruck forming with *seven* New Zealand forwards charging in to get second phase possession and, crucially, *eight* Newport forwards still on their feet to go in and kill it. When this led to a set scrum, Newport were likely to be given the put-in as the defending side.

New Zealand had two more weapons—kicks as high into the air as possible by the backs for their fast forwards to run on to, and the incredible boot of the full-back Colossus, Don Clarke. If he got a place kick within 50 yards of our line, it could mean three points against us every time.

We had answers to each. Firstly, every high ball was to be caught and marked to allow our defence to re-marshall and secondly, quite simply, we would not give Clarke a kick at goal.

That dealt with our problems from the All Blacks. Newport also had some of their own; particularly in the form of Bob Prosser and I. Bob was like myself, young, inexperienced and longing to run with the ball. He joined Newport in the middle of my first season with them, when finding a scrum-half partner for me was causing problems. Billy Watkins had lost his form, and John Morris, who now plays for Lydney, had played some games but fell out with the club. Bill Everson introduced me to a young lad from Cardiff University, Bob Prosser. We had a few passes together in training and he shone in a Newport United game to win a place in the first team. Bob had all the talents. He could sidestep, he could score sixty yard tries, he could kick with both feet, he could tackle and he had a good service.

We formed a partnership for Newport that lasted until he turned professional two years before I did. Bob was unlucky in that Clive Rowlands took the inside-half position in the Welsh team as much for his captaincy and leadership as for his ability behind the scrum and I think it depressed Bob that I and other Newport players went on to representative honours leaving him behind. At the end of our first season, we shared the Arthur Boucher cup for the most promising player which is the only time the cup has been awarded jointly.

Bob and I also teamed up off the field, talking rugby and sharing our problems, and he spent many weekends staying at my mother's before and after games. Newport's problem was getting Watkins and Prosser, the young halves to conform to the needs of the team in this vital match. If one of us got caught in possession, it could cost us the game. I had only to isolate myself once for Nathan to catch me with the ball, and the All Blacks could clinch it. For 80 minutes I was to pass only when we were counter attacking. If we weren't, the ball was to be despatched safely into touch. Bob and Dai had to be disciplined.

B.J. and Ben and Ian earbashed us so much, we began to believe it ourselves. If we conformed, the match could be won. We trained, we prepared, we rehearsed and we talked. I must have given them some anxious moments, particularly in a match before the big game when a careless pass of mine cost us a 14-3 defeat by Gloucester, but how good the plans and the preparations were is proved by the pattern of the match. It went exactly to plan and no one Newport player stood out. The team played as a team and the victory was a team victory. To the club as a whole went the ultimate honour which is how it should be.

The morning of the game I arranged with Bob that I'd pick him up at his flat in Newport to go to the ground an hour and a half before the kick-off. I was so tense and so excited that from that day to this I can remember nothing from the time I called at Bob's until after the ball had been kicked off. My mind is still a blank. I can't remember changing, or warming up or even running on to the field. For that two hours I must have been missing heart beats all over the place. If I'd been given a cardiograph by a team doctor, I'd probably have been rushed into hospital instead. Yet, I can remember the game itself vividly.

From the kick-off we played to the plan. When I got the ball, I used it to pass or kick, kicking either to touch or to get the 17 stone Don Clarke running and turning on the slippery ground. In the line-outs, Brian Price's catching technique earned us our share of the ball. If the All Blacks won possession and peeled, B.J. and Dick Uzzell unceremoniously dumped Whineray or Nathan on the muddy turf. At the scrums the Newport pack were so much a unit that they won the tighthead count eight to two, and when New Zealand did heel, our back-row of Keith Poole, Glyn Davidge and Alan Thomas created havoc with their backs. Earl Kirton was in his first game at first five-eighth and Alan 'Algie' Thomas ruined his confidence for the rest of the tour. Wherever Kirton went, Algie was to follow. By the end of the game, he must have thought Algie was a part of him.

For eighteen minutes, we had them going backwards and they looked increasingly vulnerable. Then there was a loose maul on the stand side of the field. Ian Ford, who was playing like a man inspired, ripped the ball away and gave it to Bob. Bob passed to me and I worked a dummy scissors with B.J., leaving me an outside gap to sprint through. I ran to the right, arced past Ian Macrae and Pat Walsh as they came forward to intercept me and as Ralph Caulton came in to tackle, I fed Stuart Watkins. Stuart strode down the touchline in style and when the All Blacks cut him off, he crosskicked into the centre of the field.

The Newport forwards, full of fire, were first to get to the breakdown before the All Blacks could reorganise. Briscoe and Lochore were bundled out of the way and we won possession. Back came the ball to Bob, I went one side to take the pass but Bob sensed an overlap on the other wing and passed to Dickie Uzzell. Dick ran a few yards with B.J. and Dennis Perrott outside him ready to go over for a try. He stopped and to my horror tried a drop at goal. It was drizzling, the ball was wet and it was not the day to try drop goals. Ian Ford's arms went up in despair, I half choked and B.J. screamed at him. Then we suddenly realised the ball had gone over the bar and we were three points up. Instant forgiveness. Now we knew we could win; we sensed it and the crowd sensed it. We went on with our plan, growing in confidence every minute. The menace of Don Clarke was subdued because we never conceded a penalty. Rodney Parade must be the only ground in the world he has played on without getting a kick at goal. Clarke's starvation is symptomatic of the discipline the whole Newport team showed.

In eighty minutes there was only one lapse of concentration, just one moment when the discipline broke down and over-confidence got the upper hand. I was the offender. As the cheering, the chanting and the noise of the crowd singing us home grew in volume, with a few minutes to go, Bob threw me a pass. As Nathan and Tremain came at me I had time to pass or kick as I had all through the game. Instead, I reverted to type for a moment, hesitated and side-stepped Tremain only to be floored by Nathan. In poured the All Black forwards, winning the ball and rushing off down the field. My heart was in my mouth—my one mistake and we could lose because of it. They made about fifty yards downfield until Ray Cheney answered my frantic silent prayers and scrambled the ball into touch. Almost before the line-out had formed, referee Gwynne Walters blew his whistle and it was all over. Newport had won.

Rodney Parade went mad. The crowd invaded the field. I threw my arms round every black and amber shirt I could see, and somewhere to my left, B.J. with tears running down his face was hoisted aloft by Dickie Uzzell who shouted 'You've done it, you've done it, you old bugger!' We were lifted in the air, carried, cheered and pounded on the back. It took us half an hour to get to the dressing room. There Bob and B.J. and I stood on the table, arms round each others necks while the crowd outside chanted 'We want the team, We want the team.' As I sank on my chair to take my boots off, I kept pinching my leg in case it was all a dream. I don't think I really believed it until next day and I could read the result in the papers. Nothing has ever surpassed that day for me.

The All Blacks were magnanimous in defeat. They congratulated us warmly, and admitted we could have won by much more than three points on the run of play. Their sportsmanship was excellent for even the post-match dinner and dance turned into adulation for Newport. We had to keep going out on a balcony to acknowledge the cheers and the shouts and the singing. We even heard later that supporters had linked arms across the main street in town and stopped the traffic. The enthusiasm was so great it gave us the eerie feeling that on that day we had become immortals.

I became jealous of the feat thereafter. No other side must beat the All Blacks unless I'm playing for them. No one must take Newport's victory away. In fact, Bob Prosser and I went to see them play the Western Counties at Bristol two months later. In the first minute, the New Zealanders were five points down, and after 25 minutes, eight points down. As all Gloucestershire roared their side on, we were the two solitary Welsh voices who cheered for the All Blacks. That they eventually won 22-14 sent us home happy.

There was only one other All Black defeat which would have actually pleased us—if Wales had beaten them at Cardiff. History was in favour of Wales. New Zealand had never won against Wales at the Arms Park. Wales had beaten them in 1905, in 1935 and in 1953 and only lost in 1924 at Swansea. Regretfully, history and tradition was not enough when it came to the crunch.

Four Newport players, Dick Uzzell, Brian Price (who was made pack leader), Alan Thomas and myself, were selected for the Welsh game, Algie and Dick for their first caps. Unfortunately, what a club side can do in preparation and planning was not possible then for a national team. There was no squad system as there is now and we had little chance of matching the cohesion of the All Blacks.

We met on Thursday, trained together lightly on the Friday and played on the Saturday. We needed much longer. I doubted whether the All Blacks would succumb again. I felt they had learned a lot from Newport's win and would be absolutely determined to win against Wales. It was *the* match of the tour for New Zealanders all over the world and they knew it.

Within the framework of international board rulings as they then existed, we did our best. Clive Rowlands, my partner and captain worked out a plan and tried to instil a sense of confidence in the side. A film of the Newport match was shown on the Friday evening and Brian and Alan figured largely in pre-match discussions on the importance of putting New Zealand under pressure. Alas, the best laid plans of mice and men...

We lost 6-0 but it could easily have been 12-0 or 15-0. We never got into the game. It all seemed to go wrong from the start. Conditions were abysmal, bitterly cold and the ground frozen solid. The All Blacks have been criticised because they failed to score a try but their plan was clear from the start. They were sufficiently disciplined to make few mistakes themselves, and they could exert so much pressure on us that we made the mistakes. If a Welshman was panicked into error, they knew Clarke would convert it into three points.

The first line-out of the match did nothing for our confidence. Wales were penalised and from sixty yards Clarke hit an upright with a force that shook the woodwork. Bob Morgan of Llanelli who was playing on the wing stood next to me under the cross bar. 'Christ,' he said 'one mistake, and we've had it against this fellow.' He merely voiced what we all felt and by the gasp from the crowd, it was what the spectators thought too. Five minutes later, Dai Hayward was caught offside at a wheeling scrum and Clarke put them three points up. Before half-time, he rattled the post again from the halfway line.

Wales undoubtedly had their moments. From a long throw in, I slipped Graham and had a run down the centre of the field for fifty yards but got isolated from my support. Dick Uzzell made a glorious centre break and ran for forty yards only to throw Brian Price a bad pass a few yards short of the line. At times in the first half, Cunningham, Pask, Dai Hayward and Brian Thomas looked as lively in the mauls as the New Zealanders. The fire died out later and it was All Black aggression which carried the day. The Meads brothers and Whineray were outstanding. Colin Meads was to be criticised after the game for a charge at Clive which damaged a nerve in Clive's spine. I shall have more to say of Colin later in this book but in my view it was no more than an unfortunate accident and one of which we would have heard little if Wales had won.

The second New Zealand score, a dropped goal by Watt, was hardly necessary. We were already a beaten side, and the bravery of a rearguard action in the closing stages of the game was small comfort to the capacity crowd who had come to see us win. We were depressed, of course, but defeat at the Arms Park was not new to me. Playing on a losing side was how my international career had started.

# 5. FOR ME MY FIRST CAP... FOR WALES THE WOODEN SPOON

That first season with Newport in 1961-2, with its twin excitements of my making the Newport team and of Newport winning the club championship, had brought other bonuses. Not only did I receive an invitation to play for the Barbarians, mostly I think because Brigadier Hughes of the Barbarians had watched me have an outstanding game at Blackheath, but I was also picked for the Whites in the first Welsh trial at Tredegar. This was as early in the season as November 4th and naturally there were some conclusions reached in the press that I was too young and inexperienced to play for Wales. I couldn't do much about my age and I felt that I could hardly get international experience without playing in internationals. Even so, I could see that I had a long way to go before I could clinch a Welsh cap.

In the Tredegar trial, my opposite number was Geoff Davies, who having lost his Newport place to me had gone to Cardiff. I was partnered by Tony O'Connor of Aberavon who went on to tour with the British Lions in 1962. I made two good outside breaks and came off well enough to be selected for the second trial at Bridgend in December.

This time, the other fly-half was Alan Rees of Maesteg who played so well that I knew before the game was over that I wouldn't make the final trial or the Welsh team. Any disappointment I might have felt was forgotten in the Newport performances in the rest of the season. Time anyway was on my side and in the final international against France in March, Clive Rowlands and I were selected as reserves. Wales did not play Ireland that season when a smallpox epidemic in the Welsh valleys led to a postponement until the following November. Alan Rees having turned to rugby league, the selectors reverted to Cliff Ashton for the Irish game. Wales drew disappointingly 3-3, and one felt that Wales would be looking around for a new team for the 1962-3 five nations championship.

Welsh rugby had to endure a nine-week freeze-up in one of the worst winters for years. There was a tour by a Canada XV and I played in a Wales Under-23 XV which beat them 8-0 at the Arms Park. Due to my inexperience, I neglected my kicking and ran with the ball, fortunately to some effect. I learnt one painful lesson when I held the ball too long and was laid out by the Canadian full-back Burgess, but I must have done enough to justify a selection for the postponed and only trial before the first 1962-3 international proper, which was against England. The original venue at Swansea was deep in snow so I had the advantage of playing very much at home when the game was switched to Rodney Parade a week before the England game. Clive and I were partnered in the Probables team against Richards and O'Connor in the Possibles.

I'd never met Clive until we sat together in the reserve stand at the French game but we got together in the limited time available before the trial. Clearly the selectors were thinking of us as a pair and we needed to do something about it. Casual as it may sound now, we met a few times at Clive's school in Cwmbran and practised throwing passes to one another. There wasn't much else we could do.

In the trial, we seemed to complement each other, but we lost to the Possibles 5-0 despite the warm support I was receiving from the Rodney Parade crowd. To add to the drama of the occasion, the nearness of the England match led the selectors to say that they would announce the Welsh team at 8 that very evening in the clubhouse. Three hours to wait, and the memories of my youth selection came flooding back to me. Every room and every bar in the Newport clubhouse was buzzing with rumours and arguments. I stood in the corner of an upstairs room with my family and waited, with my mind in a turmoil.

At 8 the buzzing stopped as the intercom system on the wall crackled. 'Gentlemen, the chairman of the Welsh Selectors, Mr Cliff Jones, will now announce the Welsh team to play against England at Cardiff Arms Park on January 19th, 1963.' It was so quiet, it seemed an archangel had descended.

No archangel could have brought gladder tidings. 'Outside-half—David Watkins!' The roof of the clubhouse came near to being lifted. Every Newport supporter seemed to be there and cheering his head off. I was surrounded by well-wishers, friends, relations. It was pandemonium. I shook hands with so many people that my hand felt it was dropping off. Journalists crowded around for quotes for the Sunday papers and the whole scene was so noisy and confused that it wasn't until next day that I knew Clive was in as captain, the first time Wales had selected a first cap captain for nearly 40 years, and that my youth colleague Denzil Williams, and Dai Hayward, Brian Thomas and Roger Michaelson were all in for their first caps too.

Clive and I spent the week before the match alternating between training sessions at his school and at the Rodney Parade ground where the Newport club were not only good enough to put the floodlights on specially for us but also spread straw on the frozen ground to save the skin on Clive's knees. Can you wonder that I still have so much respect and gratitude for the Newport club? That Clive and I would be playing 14 consecutive games for Wales naturally never occurred to us.

On the Friday we attended the official training session and received our instructions for the Saturday. Six new caps included or not, there were no plans for us to stay together in Cardiff that night. We were issued with our two W.R.U. complimentary tickets, our shorts, our socks, our instructions for claiming expenses and our agenda for the Saturday, and told to report at 12 next morning for a light lunch at the Royal Hotel.

Dai Hayward had said he would come up to Blaina in his car and pick me up, the idea being to share our nervousness at our first appearance for Wales. As I would otherwise have had to get a taxi all the way to Cardiff or travel on the train, I agreed. A 7 a.m. start wouldn't have been too early for me. I was in such a frazzle, that night I hardly got any sleep anyway. 'Don't worry,' said Dai, all calm, 'I'll pick you up at 9.30.'

I thought we needed to leave at 9 to be sure of being on time but he was so confident, I didn't want to make a fuss. I was up next morning at about 6.30, I shaved, washed and changed ready for what seemed the most important day of my life. I collected my kit, put on my overcoat and sat in the chair by the fire as jumpy as a sprinter on his blocks. 9.30 came, no Dai, 10 no Dai, 10.30 no Dai. There had been a heavy fall of snow overnight and I was in a frenzy. I had mental visions of Sunday's headlines 'Welsh outside-half misses first match.' 'New Cap fails to turn up for big game.' In sheer panic, I walked down to the main street in Blaina and somehow begged a lift with a carload of Welsh supporters bound for Cardiff. Breathing a huge sigh of relief, I walked into the Royal Hotel with ten minutes to spare.

Five minutes later, an unruffled Dai Hayward walked

into the hotel having had car trouble en route. He had called at the house to find me gone and still driven all the way to Cardiff in time. Amusingly enough, my parents who only knew him as the Cardiff wing-forward who had dealt very vigorously with me every time they'd seen him and compounded the 'offence' by being an hour and a half late, had greeted him with open arms and offered him a quick cup of tea. Dai drank it and then drove to Cardiff. That was Dai all over.

In many ways, he was ten years before his time. Playing now, he would establish himself as one of the great back-row forwards of all time. He could get to the breakdown for second phase possession which now counts for so much. Sure, he could be robust and, sure, with a referee who wasn't watching the offside he was the original amber-gambler. As a footballer, I still have the utmost respect for him.

Later in my union career, I could beat Dai and I tended to extract the last ounce out of doing so. Having beaten him once I wanted to go back and do it again. A very irate Hayward came off Rodney Parade after a Cardiff game when I'd left him flat on his back a couple of times and warned, quite seriously, never to do it again! I took it as a compliment! Dai was trying psychological warfare therefore he must be worried about me, not *vice versa*. Verbal warfare is the last thing one need worry about, it gives you the upper hand.

Although England had brought in seven new caps for the game, there was still the thrill for me of trotting out to face players like Richard Sharp and Peter Jackson, players towards the end of their careers but with a tremendous reputation behind them. When Richard Sharp recorded in his book later that he thought that I was 'the one man who must surely be the best fly-half the world has ever known', I was deeply touched if a bit sceptical.

One emotional experience was denied me. The Arms Park had a frozen surface like Queen's Ice Rink and with the temperature around freezing point after sixteen degrees of frost in the night, it was agreed that the teams should stay in the dressing rooms for the National Anthems. Consequently, I had to start my first Welsh international without any *hwyl* induced by *Land of My Fathers* sung by the Arms Park crowd. For the first three minutes, it looked as if we didn't need it.

Wales went off like we meant business. Robert Morgan dropped the ball after Clive had kicked cleverly, Dewi Bebb dropped a sitter after a long pass by Clive had set a movement off, and Alun Pask fumbled a pick-up. Three golden opportunities lost but with such cold hands it was not surprising. At least we were the ones creating the chances.

Completely against the run of the play, England scored. Mike Weston took a gigantic throw-in from Roberts, ran and fed Phillips his co-centre, Phillips and Jackson switched passes and places to fool Grahame Hodgson at full-back to put Phillips in from 25 yards. Dickie Sharp converted and we were 5-0 down. A quarter of an hour later we were unlucky when a loose ball on the Welsh line was missed both by a slipping Hodgson and a sliding Phillips only for Coventry's Owen to ground it. Dickie Sharp converted for 10-0. We replied with a Hodgson penalty but Sharp restored the lead with a drop goal.

I made one run for 50 yards from my own 25 but it was Robert Morgan's turn to drop the ball when I passed to him. Eventually, we did score when Dai Hayward collected at the back of a line-out and dived over the line. 13-6 and that's how it finished.

I suppose we were an inexperienced and over-eager Welsh side and lost the game as much as England won it. We were disappointed to lose, particularly against England, but the game was so much an ice ballet rather than a football match that we were comparatively kindly treated by the press. Clive had looked a convincing captain—'shrewdness and purpose personified' said Vivian Jenkins—and I was generally felt to have earned a second chance.

If we were kindly treated for losing to England, we were crucified for winning against Scotland. It was called 'the ultimate in non-handling rugby' and J. B. G. Thomas dubbed us 'the all-kicking, all static Welsh XV'. I plead extenuating circumstances. In eighty minutes, I had only two passes and there were 111 line-outs. Clive who had won the team's respect as captain, so much so that he was dubbed Little Napoleon or, more commonly, Top Cat, decided that the Welsh slide had gone on long enough. We had to win and we trained hard knowing it. The Welsh bogey of not winning at Murrayfield for ten years loomed large. Clive said that if he had to kick all day to win, he would kick all day. I suppose there were others in the side like myself who would have liked to see a fast open attacking game but Clive had the absolute loyalty of the team. We all knew that if we won, we might keep our places against Ireland. When Clive in his speech at the post-match dinner said that we came up to Scotland to win, and having won we would go away a happy team, he spoke for us all, and, I suspect, for the 10,000 Welshmen who'd travelled up to see us win.

I don't want to sound boring on the theme but winning the match was the crucial thing; and the team was more important than the individual. Apart from my two passes, I collected two drop-outs and put those into touch. It was joked in the dressing room after, that the W.R.U. should have supplied me with a pair of woollen gloves with the rest of my kit, but I'm not complaining.

Tactically, Clive was brilliant. We were getting possession from the line-outs, therefore we kept kicking to touch.

THE BIG ONE: One of the better Welsh moments as Robert Morgan evades a 1963 All Black tackle and prepares to pass out to me.

SUDDENLY IT ALL CAME GOOD: Through the gap for a try against Ireland in Dublin in 1964, and my best international performance to date.

Day of Days (1): I make one of my few attacking runs for Newport against the 1963 All Blacks.

Day of Days (2): Who says outside halves don't tackle? I prepare to stop Wilson Whineray and Co.

DAY OF DAYS (3): The heroes. *Back Row* David Jones, Keith Poole, Glyn Davidge, Ian Ford, Stuart Watkins, Neville Johnson, 'Nick' Carter (match secretary). *Middle Row* Dennis Perrott, Grham Bevan, Brian Price (capt), Brian Jones, Ray Cheney. *Front Row* Alan Thomas, D.W., Bob Prosser and John Uzzell.

DAY OF DAYS (4): The move that brought the drop goal as Bob Prosser comes away with John Uzzell, Brian Jones and Dennis Perrott outside him.

TRIPLE CROWN CLINCHER: Over for a try against Ireland at Cardiff in 1965, despite a drive by Hewitt of Ireland.

MY FINAL INTERNATIONAL: Chaired from the field by the Arms Park crowd after the 1967 match v England.

WHAT A WAY TO GO!: The Arms Park s board tells its own story of the fifty-five thriller.

Grahame Hodgson kicked a penalty and Clive (from a line-out!) dropped a goal. 6-0 and sweet victory it was too.

Reflecting on our bad press, it does seem to me that Scotland got off very lightly. It takes two to tango and they tried to play it just as tight as we did. In fact, Shackleton in the centre for Scotland didn't touch the ball until the match was three parts over. We lost the set scrums 25-13 yet Scotland were just as concerned as ourselves to keep the ball in the forwards.

An interesting sidelight to the dourness of the Scots came in an incident after the match. My father and uncle had travelled up to Murrayfield by car and on the return journey the car overturned. Fortunately, no one was hurt but as they were extricating themselves from a snowdrift, they were assisted by some Scotsmen who pulled up alongside. The Scotsmen helped them right the car, dusted them down and made sure no one was injured. They left with a parting shot:

> 'We saw that youse was Welsh, we wid nae ha'
> stapped if youse had been Sassenachs!'

The joy of the Murrayfield victory was short lived for we lost 14-6 to Ireland at the Arms Park in March. It was the first Irish win at Cardiff since 1932 and it was the first time I'd tangled with a really defensive outside-half. Mick English lay up on me all the time so comprehensively that he didn't need the assistance of a wing-forward. It was a rude awakening to the class of international rugby, in having a player who could be on you so quickly. His kicking in attack was exemplary, and the Irish tackling was quite ruthless when we tried to open out in attack. I began to solve the problems in the end and salved some Welsh pride with a couple of breaks, followed by a 40 yard dropped goal. One of the breaks was a dummy scissors with Clive, a move that we'd rehearsed and which came off perfectly. Only a desperate Irish tackle saved a score.

I still had my problems. Vivian Jenkins reported after the game that 'despite some electric running from David Watkins, he showed that he is still raw in many respects by the way he was unable to finish off his movements'. I think this is exactly right. Where my club centres had got to know my instinctive breaks and could follow them, it was more difficult for a centre in the Wales side who might never have played alongside me before. One might argue that it was their job to follow the man in possession but I had an inability through inexperience, to help them find me.

To clinch the wooden spoon for Wales for the first time since 1949, we lost 5-3 to France in Paris. It was a fast, open contest and although the whistles, jeers and other eccentricities of the French crowd did not upset me, I couldn't get into the game. Michel Crauste saw to that. The French were so quick and so spontaneous, I didn't know if I was coming or going half the time. It should have been my sort of game yet it wasn't. Clive's tactical genius was, I think, hampered considerably in that first season by not having a squad system. If we could have learned each other's games more thoroughly our record of one win and three losses would have been considerably improved. There was a lot of talent in the side and we could have taken Ireland and France.

With the nine-week freeze up and a vigorous season in Welsh club rugby that saw 69 players sent off in the year, I had a lot to reflect on. I had kept my Welsh place but I was finding the going increasingly hard. To the clubs I'd carved up the previous season, I was now the first man to be stopped. I hadn't learnt the arts of tactical kicking and when I ran instead, was tackled for my pains. The pressure was on me.

Although very few people knew it at the time because I kept it strictly to myself, I had a lot of personal problems weighing on my mind. My early marriage had not worked out properly and there was a permanent separation shortly after. Rugby may not have been going as well as I would have liked but it still saved me from the depths of utter despair to know that I could run out on to the field on a Saturday and for eighty minutes leave personal difficulties behind. At least my rugby problems were strictly problems to do with rugby.

Newport lost one game 20-0 to Llanelli when every time I kept the ball I was tackled, and every time I kicked I seemed to find a Llanelli defender. By the end, Bob Prosser and I were almost in tears—we thought the end of our rugby careers had come. We spent the rest of the weekend at my mother's afraid to go through the front door in case someone saw us and wanted to talk about the match. I was finding out how tough it could be at the top.

# 6. JOINT CHAMPIONS

The disappointing results of the 1962-3 season did not prevent the Welsh selectors from persevering with Clive and I in the following January for the trip to Twickenham. They made four changes in the team that lost to New Zealand; Denzil Williams regaining the place he had lost through injury, John Mantle replacing Dai Hayward for a first cap, and Bradshaw of Bridgend and Weaver of Swansea winning their first caps at centre and wing.

I had played at Twickenham before, for Newport against the Harlequins, but I knew there would be a great difference between playing before a small club crowd scattered around the ground, and those gaunt grey stands packed with 70,000 people revelling in a big match at the headquarters of rugby.

The social arrangements made for the Welsh team by the English Rugby Union were, as always, admirable. We travelled up on the Friday and stayed at an excellent hotel just off Oxford Street. We were taken from the train at Paddington directly to the London Welsh ground at Old Deer Park for a training session and in the evening were taken out to the theatre. Away matches always had this appeal of players being together for three days instead of dispersing every night and going home. It helped you feel so much more part of a team.

On Saturday there was a light lunch at a swish hotel in Hampton Court. This was really something, a great baronial-style dining hall full of atmosphere. Surrounded by oak panelling and chandeliers, we ate, according to choice, a steak or an egg to fortify ourselves for the afternoon's exertions. There was one bizarre exception. As the rest of us tucked in, the more abstemious Brian Thomas sat with his usual pre-match fare—a vast bunch of black grapes in one enormous hand and a glass of milk in the other. Thomas the Grape in those august surroundings looked very comic.

We went by coach to the ground and walked into the plush dressing rooms with their individual baths for every player. We always suspected the grandeur of the pre-match arrangements was partly aimed at injecting a feeling of inferiority into the rough Celts who were only up in town for the day. It had the opposite effect, always. We stepped on the field with the inner determination that we'd show them who were so bloody superior when the heat was on.

Our discussions on the train, at the training sessions, and in the dressing room had dissected the English side from front-row to full-back. Top Cat Rowlands gave us another tirade and we trotted out on to the field.

Mentally prepared or not, we were six points down in as many minutes. Grahame Hodgson was tackled when he fielded a blind side punt by Horrocks-Taylor and Ranson went over in the corner. Next our blind side defence was caught napping again for David Perry to score a try. Fortunately Willcox, the full-back missed both conversions and a subsequent penalty, or we could have been 13 points down before we pulled ourselves together. Before half-time, Clive fed me from a scrum, I broke past Budge Rogers and the ball whipped across the threes for Dewi Bebb to sprint in to the corner. 6-3 but Grahame Hodgson missed the conversion.

I had a hand in the equalising score but I can't claim

much credit for it. I tried for a drop goal, sliced the ball badly and Ken Jones got to the spot to feed Dewi who sped in again for 6-6. Grahame again failed to convert.

Without the slightest idea that it would subsequently cost us the Triple Crown, Grahame also missed a sitter of a penalty in the dying seconds. He was criticised for this but what is not generally known is that because he was suffering from a damaged shoulder, it was another player who was originally asked to take the kick. When he refused Grahame was left to do his best.

It had been a fast exciting game without touching great heights and we celebrated the draw with an official dinner and dance at the Mayfair Hotel, and an unofficial celebration on Sunday's train home. Now for Scotland.

Scotland's form up until the Welsh match had been impressive. They brought an unchanged team to Cardiff after a win over France and a hard earned draw against the All Blacks. Laughland scored a try in the first half for them when we were over-eager but the second half was all Wales and we won convincingly 11-3. Clive belied his kicking reputation with a superb break from the scrum to give Bradshaw a try which Keith converted himself. Keith followed that with a penalty and Brian Thomas scored direct from a line-out to crown a fine personal display in the second-row.

The game brought my Newport colleague Stuart Watkins his first international cap. Stuart was a complete enigma. When he was sufficiently steamed up and motivated he was the finest, fastest and most complete wing three-quarter in the world. The only person who prevented him being so consistently, was Stuart himself. His casual approach when he lost interest could be maddening. He probably thrived more on the stimulus of the big occasion than anyone, and ordinary club matches sometimes seemed to bore him.

His conflicts with the Newport club were well-known and culminated in them taking the unprecedented step of sacking him. Before that, he had stepped out of line and I, and others, had pleaded and persuaded the committee not to suspend him. Whether knowing that his status was in danger, or even because he was grateful, he scored 12 tremendous tries in the next few matches. If only he could have sustained that sort of application.

On one occasion, he failed to turn up for an important club match at Llanelli and because our reserves had been delayed by a railway derailment, Newport, a first class club, had to borrow a player from the stand. To add insult to the injury, Stuart had been seen spectating the same afternoon at a Cardiff match. To me that was tragic.

As a Welsh team we were gaining in confidence but I was still uncertain about my own game. The selectors, the other players and the Welsh public had been very loyal but I felt I had only been showing glimpses of my true form in internationals. This worried me considerably. I knew I was training hard, I knew I was trying hard, but somehow I couldn't quite produce the flair necessary to control a game. My place in the team was obviously in danger.

We went to Dublin to play Ireland. Because Ken Jones had been injured, John Dawes came in at centre. Even before John became so well known as a rugby tactician with London Welsh, he looked the complete footballer. He did nothing brilliantly and everything you asked well. Like B.J., he was a player's player and if I had been a wing three-quarter there would have been no one I would rather have throw me a final pass. After an absence lasting since 1961 my friend Peter Rees of Newport came in on the wing to replace an injured Dewi Bebb. But for these injuries, the team which beat Scotland would have been retained *en bloc*.

For me, the Irish game was the occasion when all my efforts and all my worrying paid off. Suddenly, my play seemed to click into gear and I had easily my best international to date. Against my opposite number Mike Gibson who had begun to build his reputation in the varsity match, everything I tried came off. In attack I made some incisive runs. After Keogh the Irish full-back had put over a penalty in the first few minutes, I took a pass from Clive, brushed off Gibson and hared off to the left away from the cover. I sidestepped, straightened my run and touched down from forty yards out. Bradshaw came up for the easy conversion, and although the ball toppled over as he was about to make contact he kicked it so hard it went over anyway, off the crossbar and the post. Keogh put over another penalty and we reached the interval 6-5 down. The play went back and forth and with seven minutes to go we were still down by the one point. My defensive covering was effective too and I twice brought off saving tackles when Hodgson was in difficulties.

There was an announcement over the loudspeakers that Arkle had won the Gold Cup, but that inspired us as much as the Irish—perhaps the Irish, their money safe, relaxed briefly. A long pass from Rowlands came to me. I gave it to Bradshaw cutting in and when he was tackled, the ball ran loose to John Dawes, and the man with the safest pair of hands in rugby picked it up to score himself. Keith converted. Then Peter Rees charged down a Keogh attempt at touch, Stuart Watkins gathered and ran thirty yards for another try. Keith put it between the posts and we'd won 15-6. Then we realised that the missed penalty at Twickenham had cost us the Triple Crown.

There was still the championship to be won. Another win, as it happened, could have clinched it outright but our 11-11 draw with France at Cardiff gave us a share with Scotland. As in Ireland, we left it late and were 11-3 down at the change-round, a Bradshaw penalty being wiped out by two from Albaladejo and a converted try by Crauste at the end of a long bout of passing amongst the French forwards.

Bradshaw notched another penalty and with time running out on us, Clive used a short penalty to take the French defence by surprise. The move put Stuart Watkins into the corner. Keith took the conversion and landed the goal from the touchline. 11 points all and a desperate situation saved. With this vital conversion, Keith had notched 20 points in three games for Wales.

I remember less about my performance in that game than I do about the training session at Cardiff on the Friday. When I got there the Secretary of the Welsh Rugby Union, Bill Clement handed me a letter and said, 'This should make you happy for tomorrow.' I noticed that Stuart Watkins and Alun Pask were the only two other recipients of similar envelopes and I opened it up. It was a letter from Danie Craven in South Africa inviting me to participate in the South African Jubilee Celebration matches in South Africa. At that stage, it was planned as a South Africa v The World series although later an International Board ruling forced South Africa to make the games strictly non-competitive. They were eventually played as a mixture of Springboks and other internationals in selected sides.

At any time the honour of playing with world ranked players would have excited me, but there was an additional reason for jubilation on my part. Wales were to undertake their first ever short tour at the end of the season—to South Africa. The Welsh party had yet to be announced and a bad performance against France next day could have cost me my chance of making the tour. By virtue of the generosity of the South African Rugby Union, I could get to South Africa anyway and would be there three weeks before the Welsh tour started. Stuart Watkins dropped out of the jubilee games because of a damaged hamstring, but he recovered in time to come on with Wales. When the Welsh team was announced later, Alun Pask, Stuart and I were all named, but the Craven letter was still a timely relief.

# 7. WELSHMEN ON THE VELDT

As a demonstration of running rugby, pattern-weaving and try scoring, I would not think the three South African Jubilee matches will ever be equalled. The scores 32-22, 29-24, and 44-24 tell their own story. 175 points, 34 tries, 1 dropped goal and a meagre 8 penalties—it was a long way away from truly competitive rugby. The matches were essentially artificial and tailored more to the occasion than to winning. I played in the first for Avril Malan's XV, with a South African pack and overseas backs, against Wilson Whineray's XV of overseas forwards and Springbok backs. We lost 22-32 and of course there was little emphasis on defence or on ruthless tackling on the bone hard ground. Partnered by Kevin Briscoe, I enjoyed myself and had the satisfaction of scoring a try from a pass from Doug Hopwood which sent me down the touchline and around under the posts. We were 22-16 up at one stage until Whineray's side went berserk and scored 16 more points. The spectacle probably owed more to the desire to please the crowd than it did to the operation of the new offside laws.

I played five days later in the third match for The Rest v The Presidents XV which we lost 24-44 and didn't mind a bit. At such a Jamboree, obviously, the show was the thing.

In another generous gesture, our hosts planned to present every world player with a blazer carrying a badge specially designed to incorporate, as a motif, the national emblems of the participating countries. To have so unique a souvenir of the occasion was very welcome and we were all duly measured up after the first game for our individual blazers. In what I still consider to be an extraordinary example of pettiness, in stepped the International Board and ruled that any player who accepted would be classed thereafter as a professional. This accomplished nothing, created some ill-feeling all round, but thanks to the good sense of the people on the spot I still obtained a blazer.

Quite apart from the activities on the field, the Jubilee games were invaluable to me at this stage of feeling my way in international football. All around me were world class players talking, discussing the game and forming friendships that cut across national barriers. Time and again, I found myself in a group of Australians, New Zealanders and South Africans relating their rugby philosophies. I didn't have a lot to contribute but I was all ears and came away with a wealth of vicarious experience. Rugby is remarkable for this personal basis and I feel that I could go now to New Zealand, or South Africa, find old friends like Don Clarke or John Gainsford and be assured of a welcome. Don Clarke and I roomed together throughout the Jubilee. David and Goliath, it had to be a partnership.

My Welsh accent came in for some gentle ribbing. I remember John Gainsford mimicking my voice and asking, 'Who beat the All Blacks, Dai?' and christening me Little-Dai-Who-Beat-the-All-Blacks!

After the heady delights of the celebrations, came the grim reality of the Welsh tour. They came to Cape Town having beaten East Africa 16-8 at Nairobi en route and Alun and I met up with them. I hesitate to criticise the administration of a game which has given me so much in my life, but I would be less than honest if I did not say that the tour was too short, poorly thought out and desperately unfair on the players. As if the party were a collection of diplomats on a goodwill mission, we seemed to be rushed to training, rushed off to a social function and then hurried off to a reception in the evening. I kept wanting to say, 'we're here to play rugby'.

Because we lost two of the four games, including the one Test and conceded more points than we scored, I am sure that many Welsh rugby supporters at home must have felt that we were out there for a self-indulgent junket. In the circumstances, I know we did our best. The prime purpose of any tour must be to win the Test or Tests. Even if you lose other matches, the tour has then been a success. This tour, by any definition, was a failure. I shall recount it in detail and hope that an idea of some of the real difficulties emerges.

Alun and I contributed as much information as we could about the Springbok players we had played with and against in the Jubilee games. We had councils of war with Clive the captain, the late Dave Phillips of Aberavon the Manager, Brian Price and Alan Thomas the Assistant Manager. These four made up the selection committee.

We all knew that we had a formidable task on our hands. Many of the South African players who had toured Britain in 1960-61 and lost only to the Barbarians were still playing and playing well. In fact, because of my inexperience I secretly thought of some of them as being virtually supermen. We were concerned, particularly after the first match, about the South African referees' interpretation of the new line-out laws. Brian Price was the finest line-out forward I have ever seen. Our secret weapon in Ben's catching ability was rendered null and void if he was to be continually obstructed. We even called in South African referees to explain their interpretation but it failed to clear the air. I am not saying that the referees were biased against us, I am only saying that a touring team in another country is always at a disadvantage in not knowing what is and what is not allowed.

We trained very hard indeed but time ran out on us before we could properly acclimatise. I had run one lap at altitude in Johannesburg and it nearly finished me. You had the compensation of being able to kick the ball incredible distances in the thin air but running was something else. Heat was another major hazard.

We played the first game against Boland at Wellington. I never felt that we were in danger of losing, and despite injuries to Alun Pask and John Dawes, we won 17-6. By the end of the game we were beginning to settle down and I am certain that if we had followed that game with some early matches against other sides similar to Boland over the next few weeks, we would have had a successful tour. Instead, the absurdity of the planning pitchforked us into the full Test match against South Africa only three days later and in the torrid heat of Durban at that. It was an obvious recipe for disaster.

On reflection, I can see that our tactics based on Clive's kicking abilities failed to exploit the opportunities offered by the new laws and the firm grounds, and that we neglected the match winning potential of Ken Jones and Dewi Bebb on the wings. We would probably still have lost, but nowhere near as ignominiously had we been given those extra weeks of preparation.

David Watkins had been studying the Bedford, Hopwood and Du Preez back-row menace in the Jubilee matches but they had also been studying David Watkins. I found a number of gaps opened up for me near the scrum and instinctive as ever, raced through them. Tommy Bedford admitted afterwards that the gaps were a deliberate temptation dangled for me, and once I was through them, I found myself sealed off, isolated and duly dealt with.

For three quarters of the match, we held our own. We reached half-time at 3-3 with a penalty apiece from Keith Oxlee and Keith Bradshaw. There were times in the second half when we nearly scored but the last twenty minutes were a nightmare I'd never like to relive. That I hadn't caught on to the deliberate gap tactic ceased to matter. All we could do was tackle and tackle and tackle. Dewi Bebb had said before the game that he wouldn't let Engelbrecht score. He didn't either, but the others did.

The temperature soared up to the eighties and the Springboks cut loose. As our pack wilted in the heat, we were helpless. Green jerseys seemed to pour at you from all directions. It kept flashing through my mind that we were reliving Rorke's Drift with huge Afrikaaners playing the part of the Zulu warriors. Du Preez would grab the ball and run full tilt at the smallest and weakest part of our defences—me! I grabbed him round the leg the first time and he just carried on running for twenty yards dragging me along until he was sufficiently irritated to reach down a flyswatter of a hand and brush the minor irritant off. Wilson the full-back dropped a goal from the touchline and that opened the floodgates. Marais scored, Hopwood scored, Smith scored and Oxlee converted the lot, adding another penalty for good measure.

In our forwards, Alun Pask once got stopped on the South African line and Dai Hayward sometimes got to the breakdown first, but invariably they lacked support. The real hero was John Mantle who covered superbly right to the end when the cause was hopelessly lost and we were 24-3 to the bad. If there had been any V.C.s awarded for that day, John's would have been the first citation.

After the game, we limped off the field, disillusioned and exhausted. Some players lost nearly half a stone despite a liberal dose of salt tablets, and we had sweated so much that the dye was running out of our jerseys. We could not even face the dinner in the evening until we'd rested on our hotel beds to recover.

Morale was low that night although we threw off our despondency enough to be sociable. We analysed our mistakes, realising that we'd fed the South African full-back Wilson too much. He just kicked long touches to exhaust our forwards. We worried at the bone of line-out contention again. We had normally got the throw in but Brian Price had been so hampered that we didn't win possession from it.

At this stage too, a couple of easy games could have restored our spirits and rescued the tour. Instead, we were transferred over to Pretoria to tackle Northern Transvaal three days later. This was ridiculous; Northern Transvaal was like another full Test match. The inevitable happened and we were put on the rack again to the tune of 22-9, once again at half-time being almost on level terms at 3-6.

This was one of the most frustrating games I have ever played in. It emerged before the match had been long underway that I was playing against the entire Northern Transvaal back-row. They were so anxious to hit me, that whether I had the ball or not became an irrelevance. I could see that our centres were getting the same sort of treatment and the referee either didn't see the tactics or ignored them. For the first time ever, I lost my temper on the rugby field or, if that sounds like a piece of self-deception, for the first time ever, I was caught losing my temper. It happened like this.

I got up from the umpteenth late tackle and followed a high punt to where the Northern Transvaal full-back was fielding it. He caught it and found touch. I had time to pull up, and he was much bigger than I was. I didn't pull up, I kept going and laid him low. The referee blew up and awarded Northern Transvaal a penalty. They duly put it over for three points and I was rightly lectured by Brian Price for allowing my temper to flare up to the detriment of the team. As you will have gathered, it wasn't the only lesson I learned on the tour.

The last match, only two days later at Bloemfontein, was a win over Orange Free State by 14-6 with Dewi Bebb grabbing two tries. It salvaged something from the wreckage as Orange Free State had beaten the 1960 All Blacks and held the 1962 Lions to a draw. It did demonstrate how different the tour could have been with some advance thinking in the right quarters.

In strong contrast to the goodwill shown by the South African rugby authorities at the Jubilee when Pat Walsh and Pat Love, the Maoris, were invited to liaise on the forthcoming New Zealand tour, the operations of the South African government were in depressing evidence at our four games. We were kept away from the internal workings of apartheid throughout the tour, but it depressed me to see the coloured section of the crowds herded together behind the goals. The stands were for whites only and it was noticeable that all the support for Wales came from behind the goals. In some way they seemed to look on us as their representatives and I was quite moved to think that they thought of us as playing for them.

Apartheid is now a subject much more in the world's headlines, and I have strong views about opposing it. Like most people, I do not think politics should interfere with sport and apartheid is a flagrant example of political interference with sport. John Taylor, of the London Welsh who withdrew from the Wales team to play South Africa, obviously felt strongly enough to make a personal sacrifice in order to make his own protest. In the same position I would have played, but knowing how much the withdrawal must have cost him, I have every admiration for his gesture. All possible credit should be given to him and also to the selectors for recalling him at the end of the season against France and showing that they did not hold it against him. Personally I would have played against South Africa if I had still been a union player, because many of the Springboks are personal friends and I do not blame them for their government. It is not their fault, and throughout their tour of Britain, they behaved so admirably, that they helped to show up their own government which had placed them in such a difficult position.

In 1964 we went home to Wales, sad in many ways about the tour, but I think I went back older and wiser about all sorts of things.

# 8. THE TRIPLE CROWN

However far behind South Africa and New Zealand we were, we came back to prove pre-eminent in domestic rugby. We retained our championship title in 1964-5, winning the first Triple Crown for Wales since 1952 in the process, and then clinched a championship hat trick in 1965-66.

Like a light intermezzo between the blood and thunder of South Africa and the muddy struggles of the British winter, there was the first ever Fijian tour of South Wales in September 1964. Despite distant rumblings from the International Board, the Welsh Rugby Union stood by their bold decision to issue the invitation. They were refused permission to stage a full international so the Fijians met a Wales XV instead.

I played against them in two of their five matches; for the Combined Glamorgan and Monmouthshire team at Rodney Parade and for the Wales XV at the Arms Park. What exhilarating games they were! In both cases the Welsh forwards could have played it hard and tight and won comfortably if meagrely. Against the flair and abandon of the Fijians this would have been churlish so we decided to match them at their own game. Glamorgan and Monmouthshire scraped home 23-22 in scenes of great enthusiasm. The teams scored five tries apiece but a new place kicker clinched the result by converting four of our tries. I had found a new role as Watkins the Boot and when I played in the Welsh XV which shared fifty points in the afternoon, winning eventually 28-22, a Watkins penalty appeared in the scoreline.

Apart from the delight of the Fijian frolic in the sunshine, I felt that the two games helped me make sure of a place against England in the following January, 1965. Conditions at the Arms Park can be wet and muddy as we all know, but this time, it was like playing in the middle of the Taff. There was a howling wind, pouring rain and pools everywhere.

We played with the wind behind us in the first half, needing a big lead by half-time in case we tired in the closing stages. Our forwards won a share of the ball, but we kicked too much and too inaccurately. The ball either went over the dead ball line or was fielded by Don Rutherford. At the interval we had a miserable lead of three points from my dropped goal.

Not even the most fervent of Welsh supporters could have anticipated the outcome. Instead of flagging we got stronger and stronger. Our handling of the soggy ball was exceptional and we began to play dry weather rugby so effectively that Stuart Watkins scored two real winger's tries at the end of three-quarter movements. Gary Prothero got one too and Terry Price kicked a conversion. England could only manage a penalty from Don Rutherford and we won 14-3.

The game will probably go down in Welsh legend as Terry Price's match. This was Terry's first international, from Llanelli Grammar School practically straight into the big time. That would have worried me but it certainly didn't worry Terry. I have never seen a young player who exuded so much confidence, he did not seem to have a nerve. He strolled into the dressing room before the game, changed and walked out as if it were for a Saturday afternoon kick around. In the game, he fielded the ball immaculately as it swirled about in the wind, casually kicked it 30 or 40 yards into touch, and glanced at the oncoming English forwards as if he didn't know what they were making a fuss about. He finished the season as Playfair's Player of the Year.

Question marks remained at the end of his union career about his temperament. To my mind, Terry could have been the best full-back of all time but he was plagued with injury at a vital stage of his career. The injury seemed to upset him. He became unsure of himself and his kicking form disappeared. Perhaps if he'd had less success so early, he would have taken the later troubles and his cartilage operation in his stride.

The mud was not the only subject of post-match controversy. In Monday's papers, Geoff Frankcom, the Cambridge University and England centre, was quoted as saying that he had been bitten during the match. It was a surprise to us. There had been no mention of it in the dressing room after the game and I felt that it was an incident that owed more to a reporter's desire for a good story than to reality.

The incident did not rest there. When the Welsh team was announced for the next game against Scotland, the controversy grew. Notably missing from the Welsh second row was Brian Thomas. The Welsh forwards had been a match-winning weapon against England, and Brian Thomas had been one of the best of them. He had been looked on as a certainty for the next game.

Now Brian was quiet off the field and on it he was a hard forward. Tough, vigorous, maybe occasionally over-vigorous, but having played with him and against him, I can say categorically that he was not dirty. He is also an honourable man of considerable integrity and when he said he did not bite Frankcom, that was good enough for me.

It wasn't the first time Brian had been unfairly castigated. In the Irish match the previous season, Molloy had been felled by a punch. Brian got the blame for that, yet a slow motion film afterwards showed it to have been another Welsh forward entirely. Mostly because of that rumpus, when the biting incident cropped up, Brian Thomas appeared to be the dog with the bad name and by dropping him, the selectors condemned him. In my opinion, Brian should have been in the team against Scotland.

Even without Brian Thomas, we narrowly beat Scotland at Murrayfield 14-12 in 1965. All the Scottish points came from kicks; two penalties by Wilson and two dropped goals by Simmers. Terry Price weighed in with two penalties and a conversion for us, and Norman Gale, that archetypal Welsh front-row forward, and Stuart Watkins both weighed in with tries. It was a hard fought game, which ultimately Clive inspired us to win. It was won with the last kick of the game when Terry converted Norman's last minute try. On balance, we deserved to win but how the victory put pressure on us for meeting Ireland at Cardiff! They had only to beat us to clinch the Triple Crown themselves.

Irish forwards and Welsh forwards fought hard for an ascendancy, we were all keyed up for a do or die effort. All that is, except Terry Price. He certainly tried as hard as the rest of us, but without batting an eyelid. Just before half-time, I broke away and scored and Terry calmly made it five points. Dewi also scored to make it 8-0 but Tom Kiernan brought Ireland back into the game with a penalty for 8-3. In the early stages, we could have been landed with a deficit when John Dawes was taken off, but Alun Pask showed his incredible versatility by performing admirably at full-back when Terry Price replaced John in the threes. Perhaps Terry was enjoying himself so much in the centre, that he felt bored when he went back to full back because he suddenly took a vital hand in the game. He fielded the ball safely and as we all waited for him to put it into touch, he dropped for goal from fifty yards. It was the sort of goal no one in his first season would think of trying, but because Terry was Terry, it went straight between the posts for 11-3.

We probably relaxed a little then as the crowd began to sing. We were mistaken in doing so. Flynn scored a try and Kiernan converted it. 11-8 and five minutes left. Ireland threw everything at us in desperation, but the English referee spotted an infringement and Terry Price put the result beyond doubt by kicking the penalty. The Triple Crown for Wales for the first time for thirteen years! Clive was chaired off the field, the crowd invaded the pitch, it was a great day. We sang and we celebrated. We felt ourselves to be a great team.

To put the gilt on the gingerbread, we had only to go to Colombes, and put the French in their places. They had beaten Scotland but only drawn with Ireland and lost to England. They should be a cakewalk for us. What a rude awakening was in store. In an exhibition of individual and team flair such as I've never seen equalled, they ran us ragged. I am still convinced that we had a good team and in fairness we came back into the game to score 13 points before the final whistle. The trouble was that the French ran up 22 points before we found out what it was all about. Chasing the Boniface brothers and Gachassin around the field was like trying to catch fireflies. And if they decided to take a breather, the forwards ran rings round us instead. One just has to give them credit, they were a great side on the day. We went back to Wales to lick our wounds and reflect.

One thing that went wrong was losing the toss at the start. Crauste, the captain, decided to take the kick-off not the choice of ends. They kicked deep to our line and when we put the ball into touch, they had the first throw in. Up came the full-back Dedieu into their line, and up came Terry Price into ours to cover him. The French forwards formed two quite separate groups in the line-out. They let our jumpers collect the ball and pass it back to Clive, then poured through the gap in the middle to charge Clive's kick down. No one was behind Clive and they scored. They not only outran you, but given half a chance they out-thought you as well.

This game was to be Clive's last. He had been criticised for our failure to use our scoring potential behind the scrums and, in the last analysis, I can see some justification for the doubt cast on his tactics. He had helped to build up a formidable pack, now was the time to capitalise on the possession they were winning. What is less often said is how effectively he built up the spirit of the team and instilled a sense of loyalty in every player. This facet of the Rowlands era was demonstrated when Alun Pask took over the following season. Clive had 100% loyalty and respect from us all including Alun; and Alun got it when he took over and wanted to put his own ideas into practice. Both Alun and Clive were a joy to play under.

The first stage in the defence of our title was in January 1966 at Twickenham; England, the prime enemy, the ones we most wanted to beat. The dropping of Clive, a captain who, after all, had just led us to a Triple Crown victory, had the trains buzzing with controversy as the Welsh supporters poured in for the biennial invasion.

I was looking forward to renewing my old partnership with Alan Lewis. I knew how good a player he was, and I was sure he would be the last person to let us down. In fact, he played really well and unerringly threw me long accurate passes. I enjoyed the increased room to avoid the attentions of Budge Rogers, Bob Taylor and David Perry in the English back-row.

For once in the Twickenham series, we scored first, when Terry Price kicked a penalty. Don Rutherford cancelled it out with one for England. We began to press hard, and then Terry kicked another penalty. He had his greatest moment though when Ken Jones went off on a vintage Jones run, switching direction to send the whole English defence the wrong way. Alun Pask galloped alongside him, took the ball and hurled himself over the line for a try that sent the Welshmen in the crowd delirious. Alun got up with the ball in one hand, Terry came sauntering up, as nonchalantly as you please, to take the kick which was right on the touchline.

'Do you think you can kick this one?' said Alun.

'Kick it?' Terry said, 'Just watch this go between the sticks!'

He placed the ball, ran up, and I swear he was trotting back to his position long before the ball even reached the posts. He didn't bother to look, over it went, dead centre.

David Perry, the Bedford and England number 8, who had been injured early on, managed a consolatory try for England but we left the field winners by 11-6. The jubilation in the dressing room after the match doubled when Harry Bowcott, the Chairman of the selectors, added to his congratulations the news that we were all in for the next game against Scotland at Cardiff.

In the event we did not field the same side, as Grahame Hodgson replaced the injured Terry Price. No one could have deputised more ably. Down came the rain, and as the pitch turned more and more into a morass, Grahame gave a masterly display of fielding and touch finding with a ball like a lump of soap. Winning 8-3 was gratifying enough, but I had the additional pleasure of playing my best ever game for Wales. David Coleman on BBC television said I was like a duck skating over water. What he didn't know was that there had been a family joke since I was a child that I had an inbred duck's disease, a symptom of which was carrying my rear-end too near to the ground. The conditions on the day allowed the true duck in me to come out.

As in Dublin when I played well, I was able to control my kicking, my running and my passing to the team's advantage within the context of the pattern of play. Alan Lewis missed me out when the defence converged on me, and Ken Jones and Stuart Watkins combined down the blindside for Ken to score a spectacular try. With twenty minutes to go I made a break and did most of the running myself to give Ken a second try which Keith Bradshaw converted against the wind. The Scottish forwards piled on the pressure but they could not shake the resilience of our hard working pack. We won convincingly 8-3.

As we walked off the field, my opposite number Jock Turner who had come in for a first cap, came up to me. I had given him a rough time and he asked me for advice. I was only too happy to try to help, and afterwards, I must admit to being egotistical enough to be secretly flattered. Instead of being the young Watkins seeking advice from older players, I was now in the other role myself.

It would have been pleasant to record that I and the Welsh team went on from the strength of the Scottish win to another in Dublin; but not for the first time, and I strongly suspect, by the fate of Gareth Edwards' team in the 1969-70 season, not for the last time, the Irish dashed Welsh hopes of another Triple Crown. It was true to type. We had everything to gain and they had nothing to lose. We could replay the game and win it nine times out of ten, but the crucial thing is that one cannot replay. I do not begrudge them their victory, we thoroughly deserved to lose because of our inability to win. How like rugby that is, my best international immediately followed by my keenest disappointment.

We started impressively, but without scoring. Then Mike Gibson dropped a goal. First blood and psychological advantage to Ireland. From then on it was always an uphill struggle. Gibson added a penalty and the more we worried, the worse things became. I punted into the corner and Gary Prothero scored, but Keith Bradshaw missed the easy conversion. It was that sort of day.

In desperation I tried to get a movement going from behind our line. I threw a bad pass to Ken Jones who was not even looking and Bresnihan pounced on it for a gift try. A very late penalty by Keith Bradshaw did not affect the result.

It added up to a 9-6 defeat and no Triple Crown. We went away infinitely depressed at doing ourselves less than justice.

Perhaps this defeat was looked on as a temporary aberration because when the Lions team to tour Australia and New Zealand in the summer of 1966 was announced, there were eleven Welshmen in the party. I did not immediately assess the strength of the party or think of the omissions and inclusions in the controversial selections. I thought of only one thing, I was one of the lucky eleven spending four and a half months on tour and would be having return contests with the formidable All Blacks on their home ground.

For the moment however, my mind had to be concentrated on the job in hand which was to retain our Champions' title. Our reputations already tarnished by the Irish, we had to beat France at Cardiff. I thought back to the humiliation of Colombes the previous year and of the Tulle match in my youth days, so you can imagine how much pleasure it gave me to be on the winning side against France for the very first time. We won the match and the championship by a single point and our 9-8 victory could have been an 11-9 defeat but for Lacaze missing a vital last penalty.

I do not think we were lucky. In a pulsating game that had everything, I feel we took the French on at their own running rugby and beat them at it. The selectors got us off to an excellent start by selecting ten forwards, to leave out any two according to conditions on the day. This unprecedented step laid the foundations of the squad system of the future and meant we fielded a faster pack on the day than would otherwise have been possible. The victory amply justified the means.

France went off like sprinters. Duprat was obviously going to clinch the title for France on his own if he could and in ten minutes he had scored a try himself, and set up another for Darrouy. Lacaze converted the second and France were 8-0 up. How many Welshmen were edging towards the exits at that stage will never be known but they probably thought better of it when Keith Bradshaw reduced the lead with two penalties and we began to get on top.

If any one did leave, they missed one of the most spectacular tries in rugby history. The ball reached Stuart Watkins and he broke clear. At this stage he had sixty yards to run and, with that enigmatic casualness I have already mentioned, he hesitated about going. Then perhaps seeing that he had to go alone, he switched into top gear and flew all the way to the French line with the ground in an uproar. It gave us a one point lead which we held to the end. We were the champions. It was an excellent send-off for the Welshmen who were to fight battles ahead in the Southern hemisphere.

# 9. LIONS DOWN UNDER

To tour South Africa or New Zealand with the British Lions is the summit of a rugby union player's ambition. For my name to be included in the party of 30 for the 1966 tour of Australia and New Zealand, I felt to be the climax of my union career. After the personal excitement of selection had died down I gave more thought to the many criticisms laid at the selectors' door. We had all expected the successful Welsh captain Alun Pask to be selected as Lions captain. He seemed to have done everything expected of him when leading Wales, and with the possible exception of Mike Weston of England, he looked the clear choice. We assumed that for the first time a Welshman would lead the Lions.

The discussions in committee will always remain a close kept secret but any bookmaker would have laid long odds against the name finally chosen. To most people in rugby circles, the fact that the captain was to be Mike Campbell-Lamerton, who was not even the Scottish captain, came as a bolt from the blue. In the event it proved a disaster, but I cannot stress too strongly that if it had not been for Mike's outstanding qualities as a man, it would have been much worse.

When we returned to Britain after five months away, if there was one man in the party who could truthfully say that he had given 100% effort at all times, that man was Mike Campbell-Lamerton. He worked and worried so much on and off the field that he lost two stone in weight. He had the complete loyalty of us all because he did so much to earn it. It was not a successful tour but thanks to him, it remained a happy one. There was never any disloyal sniping behind his back, and however much he was blamed by the press for the things which went wrong, no one in the party uttered a word. And that includes Alun Pask who perhaps had more reason to criticise the selection than any. Alun and Mike remained firm friends.

It is easy to criticise selectors with the advantage of hindsight but even on paper, there were glaring faults in the side. We had no specialist goal kicker, an essential feature of modern rugby, and in the event this cost us a lot of points and not a few matches. Our back-row, once Derrick Grant was injured on tour, lacked an open-side specialist and we even went into a Test with three number 8 forwards. How one longed for Haydn Morgan or Budge Rogers, both left behind in Britain.

Mike's own position in a Test side looked dubious immediately. If he played in the second-row, it meant omitting either the magnificently robust Willie John McBride or sacrificing Brian Price's line-out jumping. Mike could neither compete with Alun Pask, Ronnie Lamont or Gary Prothero for a back-row place nor justifiably replace Ray McLoughlin or Denzil Williams at prop. Mike found the solution by dropping himself twice from the Test side, and one is lost in admiration for his moral courage in so doing. He should never have been placed in such a position.

I felt the selections to be a legacy of the unspoken Lions tradition that a man had to be socially acceptable as a tourist. In New Zealand it is no joke to say that rugby is a religion, and the demands made on the Lions team off the field were enormous. We were told that the original list of functions we were to attend was cut by 50%. I find this impossible to believe because I cannot imagine us ever doing more than we did. When the All Blacks come here they concentrate on rugby. If they can find time for other activities, they will, but rugby comes first. Until we think the same, we will never compete in New Zealand on level terms. To do as much for the social success of the tour as Mike did, most people would need more than twenty-four hours in a day.

We met the other Lions at Bournemouth to be kitted out and to spend a week getting to know one another. A rule was introduced that one should never room with a fellow countryman, and by the end of the week we were a sociable bunch of footballers stepping on to a plane to take us to Perth half a world away.

I have a confession to make. In the weeks between selection and the training at Bournemouth, we were asked not to play rugby. I defied orders and played. There was a special sentimental reason. If I had broken my leg in the game and missed the tour, I would probably have cried for the rest of my life, but Blaina were opening a new clubhouse and invited a Newport team to play a special match to commemorate the event. The temptation to return some of the kindness Blaina had shown me was too much. Together with a Newport team with ten first team players in it, I went to Blaina and played. The local crowd had swelled to 5,000 and I did some urgent dressing room earbashing before the game. 'If you don't go out and beat Blaina, I'll never live it down!' We won the match 11-6 with the help of my drop goal and my eighty yard run for a try. That felt great.

I felt considerably less great when we touched down in Perth. We arrived on the Tuesday to play the first match on the Saturday but due to some malignant Hong Kong germ I went straight to bed and for four days felt that I was lying at death's door. I was so ill, I could not have cared less about rugby—all I wanted was a sharp blow over the head with a mallet to put me out of my misery.

I got up in time to watch the first match against Western Australia which we won 60-3. This was a tonic for the whole party and I wondered if I would be lucky enough to play against South Australia at Adelaide in the next match. This match was played under floodlight conditions, to which I was well accustomed at Newport. Not only did I actually make my very first Lions appearance in this game, but I made it as captain. Mike Campbell-Lamerton announced the team himself and, typically, had a quiet word with me after. He assured me that he and the selection committee had every faith in me and felt I would not let them down. This did my morale a power of good because I reasoned to myself that I must now be looked upon as one of the senior members of the party, despite this being my first appearance.

In the match we had our problems. Stewart Wilson was hobbling at full-back and our only open-side flanker Derrick Grant was taken off to hospital with concussion. I kicked 2 conversions and a penalty as a makeshift goal kicker but although we won 38-11, it should rightly have been 50 with a kicker. It did not particularly matter on the day but in a low scoring game it certainly would have.

I played again in the next match at Melbourne against Victoria. By this time our rigorous training under John Robins was beginning to bear fruit and we were a fit side. For fifteen minutes we looked an efficient one too, running up thirteen points. Then, suddenly, it all went wrong. Victoria, by no means a good side, pulled themselves together and tackled everything. Their intensive marking and ferocity threw us out of our stride and although we won 24-14, the Australian press wrote us off as serious Test contenders. We had made a lot of mistakes and, in fact,

Pig Hunt: Denzil Williams, myself, Gary Prothero and Brian Price stand triumphant over a New Zealand victim. If only the All Blacks had succumbed as easily . . .

The Evils of Tobacco: or The Dangers of Cigarettes for Non Smokers. Myself, Denzil Williams, Terry Price, Brian Price, Alan Lewis and Gary Prothero in an unlikely tableau at Wellington.

IN BUSINESS: Moving into top gear against Taranaki.

Lowly Spectator: Picking myself up off the floor as Stan Meads and Hazlett thunder on in the Second Test. McBride and Lamont running back to lend assistance.

Across the Line: Even the Christchurch crowd looks pleased as I score a try in the corner in the Third Test.

Solemn Moment: Captain of the Lions in the Final Test and looking as determined as Lochore and Laidlaw.

K.O.: Aftermath of a difference of opinion with Colin Meads in the Fourth Test. Mike Gibson and the other Lions protest and start picking up the pieces.

if one thing stands out from the whole tour, it was the inconsistency of our rugby.

No one ever found the key to why, but we seemed to suffer from rugby schizophrenia. In one Saturday match we would produce scintillating rugby and the next Wednesday, the very same players who had shone four days before would be fumbling the ball, missing tackles and generally looking a poor Lions team. It was baffling because both the skill and the will to win were always there. The moral support from the non-players was invariably high and we had almost a club atmosphere and spirit going for us.

I was a spectator myself for the next game against a New South Wales Country Districts XV at Canberra. Even from the stands it was clear that the brief honeymoon period was over and that we could expect nothing but hard games from now on. For our 6-3 win the team had scars to show; Willie John McBride finished with twelve stitches in his forehead, Ken Jones was punched, and the line-outs were an excuse for barging and obstruction. Willie John was so stunned that when rolls of thunder and flashes of lightning went around the ground in the second half, he did not dare mention them to anyone in case he was the only one seeing and hearing them!

I was back for the New South Wales game which we drew 6-6. It was really another Test match, and we were lucky with the draw. It was also a game which I personally could have won had I not missed a sitter of a penalty from about 20 yards. In compensation I might have saved the match in the closing minutes when I tackled Cardy into touch when he looked certain to score. Either way it stayed at 6-6 although I was worried after the match by how much I had allowed the missed penalty to affect my confidence in the rest of my game. It was also the last match before the First Test v Australia and I was desperately keen to keep my place. This, after all, would be the big one.

A big one fitting the occasion was how it proved. On a hot day and on a ground as hard as iron, particularly on the test cricket square in the middle of the pitch (for this was the Sydney Oval), two sides fought for the ascendancy. The result was in doubt until the final whistle which left us winners 11 points to 8. During the game Mike Weston and I worked on a double stand-off basis, switching between that and inside centre in turn. The Australian back-row were less effective as a result, and I welcomed the pressure being taken off me to some extent. There was still a time when we looked certain losers. We were 5-0 down at half-time and 8-0 down shortly afterwards. Then we began to come back. Don Rutherford kicked a penalty, then Noel Murphy scored a try which Don duly converted to put us level. Back and forth went the play until we scored a superb try from halfway with half a dozen Lions handling the ball for Kennedy to get the final touchdown. I forgot a painful graze on my leg, where the skin was rubbed off on the hard ground despite a liberal application of vaseline, and which later turned septic. All that mattered was that the Lions who had been written off as serious contenders were 1-0 up in the two match series. Champagne flowed in the dressing room, and a Lions sing song left us feeling on top of the world. We felt we had given our critics an effective riposte.

Dewi Bebb and I were the only two Test players to turn out against Queensland three days later. Alan Lewis replaced Roger Young as my partner and we ran the Queensland side off their legs. I had the personal satisfaction of both being captain again and of having one of my best games. It could have been different. Early on in the game, a Queensland forward late-tackled me and I suspected I might get similar treatment all afternoon.

Gary Prothero in his first tour appearance had other ideas. He tapped the forward politely on the shoulder and said, 'Any more of that and David Watkins will be the last person you ever knock about.'

It was an appropriate time to have so formidable an ally as Gary and it worked a charm. We won 26-3.

Our last game in Australia was the Second Test. Discreetly it was never mentioned but we played it at Brisbane which is a rugby league ground. Technically that made us all professionals! If the letter of the law had been applied, the Lions party would have been considerably abbreviated before even getting to New Zealand.

The First Test had been so agonisingly close that the first twenty minutes of the second was spent with the two sides feeling one another out. We were 3-0 up from an early Wilson penalty but neither side had gained a real ascendancy. I had a golden opportunity after twenty-five minutes to make what I thought might be the crucial score. The ball went to ground on our twenty-five and I got a boot to it to hack it on. I went haring after it and booted it on again and again and again. The Australian line got nearer and nearer, I realised I had outstripped the defence, and with my lungs bursting I tapped it over the line, fell on it and lay there exhausted but delighted. The ball went on after I had grounded it but I didn't give that a thought.

As I was still on the ground, the referee awarded a drop-out to Australia. According to him I had not touched down properly. All the elation ebbed away—I did not think I could continue. It was so disappointing, I felt utterly crushed. I knew I had scored and the TV film later proved it but it took me at least quarter of an hour to recover. Not physically but mentally. Somehow I went on playing but it needed a supreme effort to get back into the game.

It took me until the interval to recover any sort of

poise, however almost immediately after half-time I added to our lead with a drop goal from a line-out and from then on we never looked back. Ken Jones got a try, I got a try, Dewi Bebb got a try, Murphy got a try and then Ken Jones added his second. Instead of the close fought battle we had expected, we won 31-0 with Stewart Wilson kicking six out of seven attempts. What a turn up for the unsung Lions, an undefeated Australian tour for the first time for sixty-odd years and Australia's biggest ever defeat. We could hardly wait to get over to New Zealand and continue our winning streak.

Mike Gibson had joined the tour the previous day having finished his exams at Cambridge before leaving for Australia. He would obviously be my main rival for the stand-off position but for all our rivalry we have always been good friends. Throughout the tour we were to discuss our common problems and to exchange views on how matches could and should be won. After the Test, he generously remarked to a press man 'The way David Watkins played, I don't know why I came!'

From the heat of Brisbane we travelled to Invercargill in New Zealand—the coldest spot on the tour. Going from one temperature extreme to another struck us as bad planning but there was no lack of warmth in the welcome which awaited us. All we did at Christchurch en route was to change planes, yet there were thousands at the airport just to see us; and when we got to Invercargill, you would have thought we were thirty blazer-clad Messiahs. Bryn Meredith had told me back at home that once in New Zealand you don't know what hits you. Deep down I had been a little disappointed that a Lions tour had looked comparatively small beer to the Australians, but here was living proof that in New Zealand at least, we were heroes. Not only was the airport packed, but there was also a ceremonial drive from the airport to the hotel in open vintage cars. The route was lined with people all the way. It was like a scene from a Pathé News film of a royal tour, and even after going inside the hotel we had to go out on a balcony to wave to the crowd. Clearly we were in real rugby territory at last.

To give some idea how New Zealanders feel about rugby, I remember Denzil Williams and I going into a bookshop to buy some paperbacks and stationery. We were carrying a couple of sheets of photostat Lions autographs under our arms. 'How much for the books?' we said. 'Nothing,' said the man behind the counter, 'if I can have a sheet of autographs.'

I had dark suspicions that in every New Zealand maternity home, there were expectant mothers, hands clasped reverently together, fervently praying that the new arrival would be a son who would qualify for a black jersey with a silver fern on it. Rugby fervour seemed to be that deep.

Affection for the new Lions, fresh from their unbeaten Australian tour was strictly an off-field phenomenon. The reception on the field was not only warm, it was downright hot. Southland came first and they demonstrated very adequately the hard, crude strength of New Zealand rugby. We were mercilessly hounded, bundled off the ball at the rucks, and held, pushed or barged at the line-outs. The Southland pack was ferocious and our pack, with McBride at number 8, was never in it. We lost 14-8 but 24-8 would not have been thought harsh. We trooped off completely disillusioned, our image shattered.

It was Mike Gibson's turn in the second match against Combined South Canterbury and he played well in a 20-12 win. He kept the place in the next match, against Otago. That depressed me a bit because it was the first time I could have been said to have been dropped on tour. Mike did as well as could be expected with a meagre share of possession but the Lions were routed 17-9. That left us feeling a bit sick, particularly when Ronnie Lamont aggravated an arm injury by staying on the field to try to rescue the situation. Ronnie, to my mind, was the finest and most courageous forward in the Lions team and we could ill afford his absence for four weeks. It was a problem that the sensible use of a substitution law could have prevented.

Three New Zealand matches played, and two lost. After the euphoria of Australia it was doubly disappointing. Personally, I thought the first loss against Southland was a critical point in the tour. How the rest of the New Zealand provincial sides, and certainly New Zealand in the Tests, would play against us had been clearly demonstrated. The New Zealand referees' ideas of what was permissible in line-outs was so clearly at variance with what would have been allowed at home that we had to take some action.

There were three alternatives. We could grin and bear it. We could complain publicly at the treatment we were getting. We could shut up and, when the referee failed to protect us, retaliate. My own view is that we should have adopted the advice freely offered from the pen of Terry McLean and got stuck in ourselves. 'When in Rome, do as the Romans do...' he said, and I agree. This is probably what a less nice man than Manager Des O'Brien would have suggested. It was not done and the problem remained under the surface until it came to an ugly head four weeks later.

# 10. CAPTAIN ... WITH THE SKIPPER ON THE TOUCHLINE

Alun Pask was chosen to captain against New Zealand Universities at Christchurch. His belief in attacking football was amply justified by the result. We produced some exciting rugby to win 24-11 and proved that we had the potential to be both entertainers and victors. Gary Prothero was back, although he was taken off at half-time, and the expert back-row play of Gary, Alun and Derrick Grant was a joy to watch. From there we went to the North Island to face Wellington.

Alun retained the captaincy but my part in the Wellington match was restricted to a few plaintive croaks from the depths of blankets and scarves wrapped around me in the stand. I had contracted 'flu and remained a helpless spectator as Wellington under Ken Gray hammered us 20-6 with the help of Mike Williment kicking three penalties. Again the lessons were clear, we might dislike the blocking, the tugging and the barging, but we were the only ones who could do anything about it. Psychologically, we were worrying about this and instead of making the hosts worry about us, we let their tactics affect our game. We should have put them under pressure.

We had plenty of scoring potential behind the scrum and if we had won even half of the possession, we could certainly match any of the New Zealand teams.

I was back for the Combined XV match at Nelson and we won 22-14. It was nothing to be proud of. I scored one of my best tries but the overwhelming memory of the game will be of our indecisiveness and of our mistakes. In addition to securing a meagre share of possession, we were wasting much of what we did get. It augured ill for the Saturday game against Taranaki and I prefer to remember Nelson for the social side more than for the rugby.

At Nelson, I participated in my first and last pig hunt. New Zealand has an indigenous, edible wild pig and at 6 a.m., myself, Denzil Williams, Gary Prothero and Brian Price, clad in shooting jackets and unlikely hats, set off with a guide and a dog to look for pigs. The guide had a small black dog which was specially bred and trained for the purpose. The dog would root about in the undergrowth and pick up a scent. He would then dash off and chase down a pig. In one spectacular, if bizarre, movement he would race in between the pig's legs and grab it by the testicles. Not surprisingly, the enraged and pained pig would emit a series of squeals and try to manoeuvre itself into a position to gore the dog before the hunter arrived on the scene to administer the *coup de grace*. In theory, very effective.

Off went our dog. There were mighty crashes in the forest followed by anguished squeals. Our intrepid four raced to the spot, dropping guns, tripping over branches and knocking each other over in our haste. Gary Prothero was first on the scene.

'What do I do, what do I do?' he shouted.

'Shoot the pig,' screamed the guide.

Gary levelled, aimed and fired. And shot the dog. The pig got away and the dog, still clearly affronted, limped home three days later.

Taranaki was our first Saturday victory. Noel Murphy captained and led the forwards in true New Zealand style. The change in approach was effective and I used the share of the ball the pack was getting to treat the game as if we were playing Taranaki in a Welsh club derby. I worked the touch as much as possible and played ten man, fifty-five yard rugby. It proved the correct approach when we won 12-9 after being 9-6 down at the interval.

I was rested for the Bay of Plenty match which the Lions drew 6-6 and was back again for the North Auckland game at Whangerai. This time Mike Gibson was put at inside centre alongside me and, particularly as this looked to be a try-out for our team for the First Test a week later, I was pleased because I now looked the man in possession at outside-half. Ronnie Lamont and Ken Kennedy were back, the conditions were of the Arms Park variety and we won by two tries to a penalty. Even considering our previous inconsistencies, we had not lost in three matches and were looking forward to the supreme test against New Zealand at Dunedin.

How we fared there is a rather sad tale, and British rugby prestige took as much of a knock as we did ourselves. They demonstrated all their strengths, we demonstrated most of our weaknesses. At the breakdown, eight All Black forwards poured in to get quick second-phase possession. At the line-outs they got away with mayhem. This is not sour grapes, because I freely confess that they were a better side who would have won anyway but the margin could have been a fairer reflection of relative strengths if Brian Price had been allowed any protection. Instead, he and others were dominated verbally and physically and Herewini got the sort of service I would have given a great deal for. The same applies for Ken Jones, who had so little ball he could hardly be blamed for our loss by 20-3. Unfairly, I thought, he did not play in another Test although he was a potential ace behind the scrum.

Because we had already had so many disappointments, this one seemed less crushing than it could have been. I still feel that my earlier point of finding a physical answer to Meads and Co. had been heavily underlined. With Fred Allen coaching and Brian Lochore captaining on the field, it was never likely to be a love-in. We needed to meet force with force, fire with fire.

I was rested for the next Wednesday against Combined West Coast and Buller but I was not exactly missed when we won 25-6. I returned, at centre, against Canterbury, a rather more formidable bunch of adversaries. Mike Weston played at outside-half and I was told that this was to give me a chance to run with the ball further away from the New Zealand forwards; this baffled me because I had had so little ball anyway that the attentions of the opposing back-row had been academic. I was equally baffled after seventy minutes of the game when Canterbury were still 6-3 up and I had hardly received a pass from Mike Weston. This is not a personal criticism of Mike, who was only playing as he thought best; but I was switched back to stand-off with ten minutes to go and we snatched a late victory by 8-6.

In the game itself, I was laid out in a late tackle, Howard Norris was comprehensively punched in the front row, McBride stopped a corker and poor Colin McFadyean had his nose broken with a forearm smash. From the stands it must have looked pretty bloodthirsty. Like most of the provincial teams, Canterbury were determined to beat the Lions and they were prepared to bend the law books to do so.

The underlying tension reached the surface that evening at the post-match function. First Des O'Brien the manager and then Jim Telfer the captain of the day made speeches which really hit the headlines. Des O'Brien said, amongst other things, '...we are heartily sick of the obstruction, stiff-arm tackling and other illegal tactics employed by the sides we have met in New Zealand,' and Jim Telfer, always forthright, weighed in with '...every match I have played in New Zealand has been dirty.' That did it. For weeks the New Zealand newspapers were full of nothing else.

Des O'Brien was in a very invidious position and he was obviously angry at the treatment we received. As I have indicated, I think this was psychologically the wrong time to speak out. If his speech had been made at the beginning of the tour, it would have been better, but I thought that to give voice to our feelings after we had lost a Test and a number of provincial games, was conceding too much to the All Blacks. To give them any opportunity to say that the Britishers were soft and too anxious to squeal was dangerous. As I saw it, we had forwards who could more than look after themselves, and to complain was to concede that the rough treatment was more than we could cope with. That in turn, was asking for more of the same. This happens at individual level; if a man hits you early on and goes scot-free from both the referee and yourself, you can be sure you will be on the receiving end throughout the game.

We beat Manawatu-Horowhenua comfortably by 17-6 at Palmerston North, a game which I only watched, but for the next match against Auckland I was selected to captain the side. Auckland were very strong, the holders of the Ranfurly Shield, and I was sure that the match would be fierce. To be honest, I was delighted to be in charge. Once I was out in the middle of the field, I could hardly pop off and consult the tour committee, so I could get the team to play it my way. In the dressing room I really launched myself into a blood and thunder bit. We were going out there to represent Great Britain, and to die for Great Britain if necessary. It will be hard. Ask no quarter. Give no quarter. We'll open up only from good positions. Win me the ball whatever the Auckland pack throw at you and we can win this.

When we got out there, it really was fierce. The Auckland pack were less than particular about their targets and just after half-time, someone threw a punch at Noel Murphy. That did it. At a line-out all sixteen forwards slugged it out for some thirty seconds and the referee had to run through a whistle obligato, with players trying to pummel each other off the park. He called myself and Nelson, the Auckland skipper together and said the next man to try anything from either side goes off. Go and tell the teams. This suited me fine, I went back and could say all right, Auckland now know they can't knock us about, let's play some football. If the referee was going to protect us we no longer needed to defend ourselves.

From then on, the game was clean, exciting and touched the heights. We notched one of our most convincing wins by 12-6. The punch-up had people throwing hands up in horror all over the world but I firmly believe it was right in the context. Auckland had to realise that we were not as soft as our publicity suggested and that there was no point in trying the rough stuff against us. After the fracas, we demonstrated that rugby was a game of skill, not brawn, and I would rate it as my best game in New Zealand.

This match must have lead to the very pleasant shock I received before the Second Test. Mike Campbell-Lamerton again proved what a great guy he was. He came up to me before the Lions team was announced and said,

'David, you are going to captain the Test side. I wanted you to know what was happening before the others do. I have dropped myself, I have every confidence in you and I hope you can pull it off. Let me be the first to congratulate you.'

I did not know what to say to him, but I hope he realised how much admiration I had for him at that moment. When it came to leading the team out at Wellington, it brought tears to my eyes and I knew what a sacrifice he had made. The rest of the team were more irreverent and a song about the qualities of Watkins 'the little Hitler' began to gain local popularity in the Lions hit parade.

Before the game I went through a similar harangue to my Auckland one. We took the field determined to do our best and if possible, to level the series. The record books show that we lost 16-12 and never crossed the New Zealand line, but that is by no means the full story. Not only could we have won, we should have.

I have never been one for criticising referees after a game but Pat Murphy, who refereed three of the four Tests, in my opinion made some errors in this game which cost us dear. We played a hard pack who matched the All Blacks in every respect and I thought we were the best team on the day. Twice we all but scored tries, once with Gibson clear, and once with McFadyean. Neither could have been caught and in both cases it would have been an easy five points. On each occasion, we were whistled up and given awards in *our* favour—one a penalty sixty yards back, and the other a scrum under the posts. Poor consolation for ten points lost.

We lost the next provincial game against King Country under Colin Meads, won an exciting game against the Maoris, just beat Poverty Bay 9-6 and drew with Hawkes Bay 11-11. In no time at all we were into the Third Test.

On the basis of our performance in the Second Test, we should have had a good chance. Regrettably, the selectors unbalanced the pack before we took the field. To get Mike Campbell-Lamerton back into the second-row without losing Delme Thomas's ability in the line-out, they chose Delme as a prop. Against an All Black pack who were experts in their various departments, this seemed suicidal. So far as I know, Delme had never played there in his life and to expect him to become an international prop overnight was desperately unfair. The Lions pack, despite the tremendous efforts of Ronnie Lamont who crowned his display with a try, never got fully into the game. We made some characteristically silly mistakes in midfield; Colin McFadyean delaying an elementary pass to Stuart Watkins when Stuart was clear, and Murphy and Bebb between them missing a harmless kick ahead to let Nathan score. And so it went on. We eventually finished 19-6 down. I had to leave the field to have an ankle strapped up but it never hampered me and I scored the second of our tries. The series was over to all intents and purpose and one just hoped we could win the last Test to salvage something from the wreckage.

I was not sure I would be in the Fourth Test. Terry McLean, among others, was pressing hard for Mike Gibson's inclusion at outside-half and Mike had played exceptionally well against the New Zealand Juniors. He moved back to inside-centre for the Waikato match when I returned at stand-off. Between us, we wreaked havoc with the Waikato defence and we ran out winners by 20-9. That restored some of my confidence.

I only watched the Thames Valley Combined match on the Tuesday before the Saturday Test. The stand was the best place, as it turned into an unpleasantly hard game. Unnecessary obstruction and late tackling by Thames Valley brought a lot of needle into it, and the match cost us three Test players. Stuart Watkins tore a hamstring, Noel Murphy cut his head in a collision and Delme Thomas injured his back. Delme's injury came in a collapsed scrum and the selectors who had persisted in the lunacy of playing him at prop must bear the responsibility. In fact, Des O'Brien manfully and publicly admitted the mistake after the game. It was too late.

Considering the injuries, we eventually took the field for the Fourth and final Test with a strong team. It had been announced at a training session with us all as tense and worried as if we had been waiting for school exam results. To hear I had passed was a relief but I was genuinely surprised to be chosen as captain again. Perhaps Alun Pask should have played at number 8 and Jim Telfer on the flank instead of vice-versa—but in Ray McLoughlin and Denzil Williams we had a rugged pair of specialist props; in the second-row we could rely on McBride and Brian Price; and with Lamont completing the back trio, we had a hard but mobile set of forwards.

History shows that we went down 24-11. Without any special pleading, that bare scoreline disguises the true differences between the teams. We would have lost but the magnificent fight we put up entitled us to a much closer result. The All Blacks scored two tries with an element of fortune about them in the first twenty minutes and converted them both. In the first we were waiting for a scrum for a knock-on by Dewi Bebb and Nathan took the ball from a quick throw in by Meads to go over, and in the second, a lucky rebound put Dick clear for another.

That left us 10-0 down but there was no collapse in morale. We were still in with a good chance but three minutes later, we suffered the real disaster. Alun Pask jumped up for the ball at a line-out, and an All Black forward pushed him over. Down went Alun on his shoulder. There was a nasty crack and Alun had to be carried off on a stretcher with a broken collarbone. Left with seven forwards for the remainder of the game, no one can say we gave up. Before half-time, we scored the try of the series when Ben Price won us a line-out. I ran diagonally switching with Mike Gibson, linked up with Colin McFadyean who gave it on to Wilson in the line and Hinshelwood got over in the corner. It was a perfect move and I understand that it has been since incorporated into a coaching film.

Almost at the next scrum, Alan Lewis robbed Chris Laidlaw and Mike Gibson put McFadyean over at the posts. This time, we converted and changed round only 10-8 down.

In the second half, we were again robbed of a score not unlike my non-try against Australia. Mike Gibson hacked on and made forty yards in a dribble, the ball bounced high and Mike pushed it on again with his knee. The referee, who was definitely unsighted, blew up for a knock-on. We had been robbed of another certain try. Mike said he did not knock-on and Mike is the sort of man who would be incapable of telling an untruth. I then missed by inches with an attempt at a drop, and just afterwards came the occasion when Goliath for once felled David.

So much has been made of Colin Meads laying me out in this match that I had better give my version. Colin Meads is the greatest second-row forward playing rugby. He is also the great referee! In New Zealand, he never seemed to stop talking and if you did not completely ignore it, this could put you totally off your game. 'Penalty, ref!' 'Offside, ref!' 'Watch that man, ref!' 'What's he doing, ref?' It got to such a pitch, I almost expected Colin to produce a whistle at any moment and award himself a penalty.

He knew all the tricks of the forward's trade, and earlier in the match he had adopted one of his favourite ploys to gain ground when we were awarded a penalty. He tried this when I was about to take a kick to touch. 'Get back and grow up!' I said, which probably went down very well.

Almost immediately from the drop out after my narrow miss at a drop goal, I collected the ball and kicked a long touch. Colin, who was running at me, did not pull up as it seemed to me he could have, but pushed me down instead. I got up and not having the sense to accept the tackle and forget it, I went over, pushed him in the chest which was about as far as I could reach and said, 'For God's sake, who the hell do you think you are?' and suggested none too politely that he four-lettered off to his own half. Colin did not deign to reply but punched me smack on the jaw instead. I went out like a light and came around a couple of minutes later.

Many of the press said that this incident marred the game and harried me for comments which I refused to give. So far as I was concerned, I didn't want to exercise my jaw which was still a bit sore, but equally I did not want to make anything of the incident. I expect no special treatment for being small. It was all so deadly serious that we sat next to each other at the dinner in the evening and had an enjoyable evening. In fact, when Colin, who I am quite sure had no intention of kicking at Chisholm, was sent off against Scotland on the 1967 All Blacks tour, I wrote a letter of sympathy to him and had a friendly reply wishing me good fortune in my new career in rugby league.

There was an amusing sequel after we had returned home. Meads apparently visited a local school and a young lad asked him. 'Please, Mr. Meads, why did you hit little David Watkins in the Test match?' Colin looked very grave and said, 'Self-defence!'

Later in the half, the strain of playing a man short began to tell and MacRae scored a try converted by Williment. Herewini dropped a goal and our cause was irretrievably lost. The gremlins had not quite finished however and there were two forward passes in a movement that put Steel over in the corner. There was a penalty apiece by Williment and Wilson, but it all added up to

24-11 and a 4-0 series to New Zealand for the first time ever.

We came home via Honolulu and Canada. The week in Honolulu was a pure holiday and foolishly I lay in the sun for hours determined to go home with an expensive looking tan with the result that I had a terrible time with sunburn afterwards. Because the Lions were so depleted by injury, I played, sunburn and all, against British Columbia. Howard Norris even played as a blind-side flanker which should give some idea of the desperate nature of the situation. We lost 8-3 and when I took my jersey off at the end, all the skin from my back came with it. I left it to the rest of the party to beat Canada 19-8, I had had enough. One old acquaintanceship I renewed was with the British Columbian full-back Burgess. Remembering that he had layed me out years before at Cardiff, he looked at me and asked solicitously, 'Are you feeling better now?' I nearly said yes, and I would be feeling considerably better if we had won at least one Test in New Zealand.

# 11. DROPPED

I had been away on tour for nearly five months. It was five months spent playing rugby and training for rugby. Despite the ups and downs of the Lions tour, I felt that it had been personally successful and I felt fitter than I ever had in my life. This sense of physical well-being I jealously guarded and I went out training on my own on the nights when there were no Newport sessions, running around the mountains at Blaina, concentrating on keeping the edge on my speed and stamina.

Mentally there was no adverse reaction to the tour in my appetite for the game. The Australians, who I'd given so much trouble out there, were the visiting tourists, and I was raring to go at them again. Just the sight of the old familiar black and amber jerseys at Newport was a stimulus to my desire to play.

These emotions were so strong that I felt that I knew in my heart, whether it sounded like a cliché or not, I could have lived and died for rugby football.

In the next few weeks I was given such a rude awakening that it brought me a timely reminder that rugby, however important, was no substitute for life.

Many people had asked me if I felt stale from the tour, and I answered honestly that I felt on top of the world. In Newport club games, I was playing well and thoroughly enjoying it. I played in the Welsh trial and was given my first introduction to the skills of a very young

Gareth Edwards. Even at that early stage, Gareth looked an exceptional footballer and full of talent. His kicking, his running and his tackling were exceptional but his service on the day was appalling. We didn't hit it off at all, and I spent the afternoon grabbing at the ball coming to me at all heights and speeds and even if I did catch it cleanly, I had, of all people, Alan Thomas marking me. Algie and I had played so many times together that he knew every trick in my book and he could have been blindfolded and still tackled me four times out of five. It was not a happy trial.

An additional embarrassment was a mediocre Newport v Australians match when two sides, equally poor on the day, served up a 3-3 draw at Rodney Parade. It was embarrassing, but I didn't think of it as disastrous, particularly when three of the Welsh selectors came up to me after the game and said, 'All right, David, we don't want you to play any more rugby now, save yourself for the international against Australia.' Now I had never voluntarily dropped out of a game for the club and I was reluctant to start. Newport had been exceptionally loyal to me and I wanted to show I appreciated it by being loyal to them whenever they wanted me. I had little option however but to withdraw for the next few games. It was a hardship because I had reached the stage when the sheer joy of playing meant more than any more honours I could win.

I heard nothing more until a week before the Australian game, when I was watching television and heard on the news that there were changes in the Welsh team. On an impulse I did something I'd never done before, I got up, walked down to a local telephone kiosk and rang Brian Wall, who, in addition to being a rugby writer on the *Football Echo* was a good friend.

I asked him, 'Is the Welsh team out?'

He said, 'Yes, David, it is and I've got some bad news for you. Barry John is playing against Australia.'

I didn't hear anything else he said. Not even the rest of the team. I put the 'phone down and walked back in a state of shock. I was really stunned. I went back and told my girl friend Jane. At first she did not believe it, and then she started crying when she saw that I was serious. I went back to my parents' house at Blaina and broke the news to them. They were upset too, and the effect on me as to how important my feelings seemed to the people closest to me, brought me to the vivid realisation that there was more to life than playing rugby. If I never played again, I had a lot to be grateful for.

I went out again and sent Barry John a telegram of congratulations. This cost me a lot, not because I disliked Barry in any way, but because it was conceding a point to a rival. Part of having a competitive nature is wanting to be better than anyone else at whatever you are doing.

Few players go through a sporting career without being dropped at some stage or other, and I would not like it to be thought that I was a special case. Nevertheless, there was something about the affair which was rather curious. I came back from the tour, on which I had been thought good enough to captain the Lions in two Tests. I was then left out of the Welsh team for the first two internationals, but for the third, I was not only good enough to play, I was good enough to come in as the new Welsh captain. It lacked logic.

However selfish it sounds, I found sitting in the reserve stand watching Barry playing against Australia, very hard to bear. He played very well and I knew he would retain his place against Scotland, although Wales lost to Australia for the first time ever 14-11. Wales lost at Murrayfield 11-5 with 6 new caps, and change was again in the air.

For the Irish game at Cardiff, both Alan Lewis and I

were recalled. I was the new captain. I took the responsibility seriously and I tried to apply my experience of captaining Newport. I talked of the importance of every member of the team backing each other up. We were all internationals and experienced players and there was no reason why individual flair should be curbed. On the other hand, if you can cope with your own job adequately, there was every reason to look for the opportunity to help out anyone else in difficulty. Ireland would be looking for the chance to cock a snook at us again. We must stop them.

Ireland took three minutes to score. Mike Gibson was the creator, and Duggan the scorer, of a try in the corner and the 3-0 lead settled them in nicely. They had the best of the first half with Alan Lewis having an uncharacteristically uncertain game. They nearly scored again when Brophy gathered a Mike Gibson punt in his stride and raced towards our line. Grahame Hodgson, who had been brought in instead of Terry Price, when Terry withdrew, must have taken my pre-match talk to heart. He flew at Brophy and crashtackled him into touch, knocking himself out in the process. It was a brave effort.

I did some more talking in the interval. In the second half, our pack climbed back into the game and we came desperately near to winning the match. If Terry Price had been fit we would have. Grahame and I shared the place kicks and missed two easy penalties each. Before the end, I all but scored a spectacular try. I broke away, side-stepped and a few yards from the line, Ken Goodall got near enough to brush my ankle and unbalance me. I fell on my nose a foot away from grounding the ball; and, for all our efforts the match was lost.

We finished the season with two games in April—the first against France at Colombes. Alan was dropped and Gareth Edwards capped. I was very apprehensive after the trial experience at the beginning of the season and went to the Arms Park to train with him. In a ground with a 60,000 capacity, there were two spectators—Gareth's girl friend and Jane. They watched us running and passing as we tried to reach an understanding. I wanted the ball to come to me accurately. If that meant a short pass, I did not mind. I would rather have it in my hands from three feet, than above my head from twenty yards. His ability being what it is, at Colombes, with our forwards on my instructions protecting him as much as possible, he gave me a sound service all through the game.

Terry Price was back but it was a new uncertain, mortal Terry Price and he missed five out of eight reasonable kicks. The old Price would have backheeled some of them over. I felt sorry for him in his loss of confidence, and I wasn't surprised when he turned professional after this, his last international.

With Guy Cambarabero, the French had no kicking problem. He notched 14 of their 20 points against us, totalling 68 out of 116 points in 4 matches. Curiously enough, I still wish one of his kicks had gone over. At a crucial stage in the match, he hit the post with a penalty and the rebound went straight into Dourthe's hands and it cost us five points instead of three. That turned the tide against us.

The lead fluctuated throughout the game. Terry Price kicked two penalties, and converted a superb Dewi Bebb try after Dewi charged down a Gachassin hack into touch and kicked the ball all the way from our 25 to fall on it over the French line. I dropped a goal. They were 14 good points but Cambarabero staged a grandstand finish; he converted Dourthe's try, dropped an arrogant goal and then flashed over for a try himself. He missed the conversion but it no longer mattered. We had lost 14-20.

With a dismal four consecutive losses behind us, a confident England had to be faced at Cardiff in the last match of the season. I had no idea then that it would be my last international, but as it turned out, I could hardly have gone out on a higher note.

One lesson stood out from our record. We could not afford to take the field without an established goal kicker. Desperate situations need desperate measures and one wondered what the selectors would do. Before the team was announced, they gave the Newport club the broadest of hints by asking us to give our new centre, Keith Jarrett, a game at full-back.

Keith had been at Monmouth school until Christmas. He was big, strong, fast and he had been kicking goals from all over the park for us at centre. Despite his enormous talent, he still had a lot to learn about the finer arts of centre play and as far as I knew he had never played at full-back in his life.

As the Newport captain, I was on the selection committee which had to decide whether we would comply. We were very loathe to play anyone out of position unless there were pressing club reasons for doing so; however without being desperately unfair to Keith, there was little we could do but agree. We switched John Anthony to the centre and played Keith at full-back against Newbridge at Rodney Parade. It cost us the game.

Keith had a nightmare. All his enthusiasm and effort were secondary to his inexperience. He did not know where to stand to cover and Newbridge exploited it mercilessly. They kicked Garryowens at him and either stampeded him into missing the ball or being tackled in possession. Before his confidence was finally shattered, I took a hard decision. At half-time, I took it on myself to switch him to the centre and put John Anthony back at full-back. We still lost the game but I felt I had rescued something for Keith out of the wreckage, and he looked a different player in the second half.

He went into the Welsh team at full-back. As captain, stifling my doubts, I tried to instil as much confidence into him as possible. The wing and the fly-half cover the full-back more than anyone else, and Stuart Watkins and I, both club mates of his, promised him all the support we could manage.

My words to the forwards in the dressing room were fierce. I went at them like a hellfire preacher. Drawing myself up to my full five foot six inches, I tried to inject enough *hwyl* to last eighty minutes. 'We are playing for ourselves, for the selectors and for the Welsh public who have paid good money to see us decimate the English enemy. Let's get out there and take them apart.' One can never be sure if this sort of talk gets over but the team looked so determined, they almost frightened me.

The first penalty we were awarded was a kick I would normally have put into touch myself. Instead, I called up Keith to give him a feel of the ball. He put it safely away and the rest of his performance is history. He kicked everything. I gave him the ball, he placed it, and over the bar they went. He missed one only and that hit the post. He kicked five conversions and two penalties and they went in from everywhere, off the posts and off the bar included. Those sixteen points would have put him permanently in the record books, but it was not the end of the story. He scored the most fantastic try that I have seen in my rugby career.

Colin McFadyean put an attacking punt into a normally unoccupied area of the field. It was a good kick and, in usual circumstances, would have spelled danger to us. Keith, miles out of position, was there. Off he went, careering down the touchline, and making the sixty yards to the English line without a hand being laid on him. It came at a stage when our original 14-3 lead had shrunk to 19-15 and the shock finished England's recovery. With all

Wales singing their heads off, we rattled up 34 points to England's 21.

The seal for me was set on Keith's feat by a story circulating the valleys later. Keith was supposed to have turned up at the Cardiff Bus Station after the post-match dinner. He waited at a bus stop for the last bus to Newport which had left ten minutes before. A conductor and a driver came past.

'Eh,' they said, 'the last bus to Newport has gone! You won't get one tonight now.'

'Oh dear,' said Keith, 'that means I'm stranded.'

'It's not Keith Jarrett is it? Nineteen points against England this afternoon?'

'Yes.'

'Hang on there, Keith boyo, we'll get a bus out of the garage and run you home.'

They disappeared and came back with a bus. Keith was just about to get on board when an inspector came up and addressed the two bus men.

'Where are you going with that bus?'

'Well, it's Keith Jarrett here see. Nineteen points against England this afternoon and missed his last bus. We're going to take him home.'

'You put that bus back now!'

'Yes, but Keith, nineteen points and stranded...'

'Put it back—and get him a double-decker, he might want to smoke!'

More in touch with reality, I spoke to Keith after the game and tried to tell him that he should not let the experience affect him too much. Keith had a well-balanced personality and was unlikely to get swollen headed, but it was worth reminding him that at any time in the future if he had an off day, his nineteen points against England would be brought up as a stick to beat him with.

As it happened, only two days later, we played together

for Monmouthshire against North Wales. North Wales beat us for the first time ever, mostly because Keith missed everything. It was, in many ways, the best thing which could have happened. That Keith had the capacity to take successes and failures in his stride is proved by the fact that by the time he came back from the 1969 Welsh tour of New Zealand and turned to rugby league, he had become a world class centre quite apart from his kicking ability.

Before I come to tell you how I came to leave the game I loved, there is another aspect of rugby union I must mention—seven-a-side rugby.

# 12. MINI-RUGBY

Sevens tournaments can be an end of season frolic, a light hearted run-around to finish off a hard season's rugby with no one taking it seriously and seventy yard tries scored all afternoon to entertain a crowd in their shirt-sleeves with their minds half on the rugby and half on their picnic hamper. At Newport we never played it like that.

Astonishing as it may sound, I got more tense and more worked up throughout the day of a sevens tournament than I did before a Welsh international against England. This was partly because of the nature of sevens. The flurried activity of two seven-minute halves would be followed by a long wait before the next one, and the anxiety of wondering who you would be playing next. To me it was a serious business. In my book, you had no business entering the tournament if you were not serious about winning it, and in the words of Brian Jones, you had no business in the final unless you won it.

The name of Brian Jones is the key to all this. At sevens, he was the acknowledged master. All his natural ebullience came to the surface, and his influence spread throughout the team. Newport had originated the Welsh Sevens in 1954 when Mr. R. S. Snelling had presented a challenge trophy to be played for. Here again Bill Everson was the pioneer and his dedication and enthusiasm made it all possible. In that first tournament, Newport, and Brian and Malcolm Thomas in particular, had wiped the floor with the opposition to be the first holders of the Snelling Cup.

When I first played sevens for Newport, at the end of my first season (1961-2), we were going down to Swansea with the pressure on us. Not only had Newport monopolised the Welsh Sevens by winning five times in the intervening eight years only once failing to reach the final, but we were also going as the new Welsh club champions.

As I have told you, I had played sevens with Cwmcelyn Youth with some success. You got the ball, you ran, you beat the man who was marking you, and you scored. If you did this more than the opposition, you won the tournament. That's what it was all about.

B.J. had other ideas. Bob Prosser and I met up at Newport Station to get on the special coach to go down to Swansea. We were apprehensive to say the least and almost holding hands to reassure one another. Up came B.J.

'I don't know what you pair are going to do with your tankards, you don't even drink.'

'What do you mean?' we said.

'Well, your tankards. You get an individual tankard for being in the side that wins the sevens.'

Bob and I exchanged glances. We had not even left Newport, and as far as B.J. was concerned, we'd already won the tournament. He went on in this vein all the way to Swansea and by the time we got there we began to feel confident that Newport *were* going to win the tournament.

If we had had the necessary sevens experience to assess our team objectively, we would have seen how strong a team we were taking. There may only be seven defenders to beat, and on the average sized rugby field, 8,000 square yards of space to do it in, but that is only half the story. You can do nothing without the ball. Possession is even more vital than in the full fifteen a side; and you have to know how to use it when you've got it.

The Newport team was worth looking at with this in mind. We had Bryn Meredith as hooker and captain, Brian Price and Glyn Davidge as the other forwards, and behind the scrum we had Bob and I, B.J. and Byron Thomas on the wing. The point is that Bryn, the best hooker in the world, could win us the ball at every scrum, Brian could take every line-out, Davidge could cover anything in the loose and when we did win the ball, the other four were all fast and all capable of scoring tries. Bryn could issue general instructions as captain, and B.J. could play a complicated game of chess with the backs, swopping them around to get a flier out on the end of a move to finish it off. When one player had run a long way for a try, he would find himself in a position to feed a fresher player for the next long run.

B.J. was not only concerned with winning a particular round. He had half his mind on winning the next one and the one after that by conserving our energies. Bob and I were like two glove puppets. We were only allowed to come to life when B.J. said so.

'Run!' he'd scream, and we'd run. 'Stop!' he'd scream and we'd stop. This had a comic side-effect in the semi-final in which we played Llanelli, having already beaten Cross Keys 8-0 and Aberavon 10-0. We notched up 14 points, a comfortable lead but Stuart Davies of Llanelli broke through our defence sixty yards out from our line.

'Stop!' roared B.J., and Bob and I, who had started to give chase, stopped. So did Stuart! He looked back over his shoulder—the Newport team was rooted to the spot. B.J. had his arms folded, totally disinterested in the proceedings and studying the architecture of the St. Helen's pavilion. Stuart walked on a bit further, ran a bit, looked around again and eventually touched down, with the Newport players still ignoring him and being roundly booed for not chasing. They kicked the conversion and the final whistle went. We had won 14-5. We went back to the dressing room to rest for the final against Neath with jeers, catcalls and boos ringing in our ears.

When we got there, Bryn Meredith closed the door. He spoke to Brian Jones.

'Do you think that's the sporting way to win a tournament in front of all these people?' Silence from B.J. 'Good man,' said Bryn, 'keep it up!'

The final versus Neath was a formality. Off went Byron Thomas for a try. Bob put Brian Price in with a little run around the scrum, and B.J. converted it. Bob added another himself and after David Richards had scored Neath's only try, I ran in from 80 yards for another. B.J., grinning from ear to ear, converted it and we'd won, 19-3. The tankards were ours.

The next season, we had to go to Cardiff Arms Park to defend the cup. We took the same side with the exception that Graham Bevan took over as hooker from Bryn who had retired. B.J. was now captain. We also took the same tactics and they were equally effective. In the first round, we beat our arch rivals Cardiff 14-5 and if the home crowd had any affection left for us, they did not show it after that. We beat Cross Keys 13-3 and met Neath in the semi-final. We came out to play Neath. B.J. put one foot over the touchline and what seemed the entire crowd of 20,000 booed. Neath, if they could beat Newport, were first in line for canonisation. No set of circumstances could have pleased B.J. better. Nothing was more calculated to put him on his mettle. He swaggered out, waving a hand graciously as if to acknowledge the cheers.

The Neath match was tough, a real humdinger. Dave Morris scored an unconverted try for them and the play went back and forth, with time running out for us. B.J. no longer had to shout and chivvy us to do the right thing, so he went to work on Neath instead.

If he was tackled, he'd get up, ruffle his opponent's hair and say, 'Well done, sonny, but don't get any big ideas.' And he'd call across to the Neath backs at a line-out or scrum, 'Now, now, don't set your hearts on those tankards. We'll win this!'

This gamesmanship so infuriated them that, in the last minute, B.J. got the ball and not one, but two Neath players ran at him determined to silence him for good. Seeing the gap, he waited until they were almost on him and slipped it to me. I had a clear run in for an equalising try.

Up came B.J. for the conversion. He strolled up, a rosy victorious glow on his face, made a few Churchillian gestures at Neath and at the crowd, and as the whole Neath team charged at the kick, he chipped it over dead centre. 5-3 and the whistle blew. We were in the final again.

After that excitement, the final against Bridgend was strictly an anti-climax. B.J. scored a try and converted one from me for an 8-0 win and another Newport trophy.

In the 1964 sevens, a Newport side depleted by Brian Price, Stuart Watkins and myself being away on the South African tour, lost 6-0 in the first round to Neath but we were back in force in 1965.

This time, I had every reason not to play. I had dislocated my shoulder in a club game three weeks before and I went down to the sevens training session with my arm in a sling. I watched the rest of the team throwing the ball about and I am afraid I could not resist it. I was now club captain, B.J. had left the club to play for Tredegar although he has since returned as joint coach, and I had to try to do a B.J. myself.

It was a silly decision in many ways, not least because it could have aggravated the injury so much that I might never have played again. I knew the risks but the sevens was so important to me that I rationalised it to myself. I

CONGRATULATIONS AND JUBILATIONS: A Union send-off for the new League player. Dennis Perrott, Bill Morris, Brian Jones and Brian Price wish me luck for the next day and my first professional game.

HAPPY BAPTISM: Haring off for Salford and on the way to my first try in rugby league.

(*Overleaf*) AIMING FOR WEMBLEY: In full flight for the Warrington defence in the Rugby League Cup semi-final at Wigan.

DRESSING ROOM EMOTION: Mr. Snape, myself and the Salford team celebrate the win over Warrington and drink a toast to a victory at Wembley.

THEY ALSO SERVE .. Colin Dixon and Charlie Bott in the thick of the Wembley action. Most of my time was spent in watching, waiting and hoping.

reasoned that whereas I would not have dared to play in a club game, it should be possible to go through a sevens tournament without being tackled. It was also selfish because I might have let the team down but anyway I played.

We were at St. Helen's, Swansea again. I told the team that eleven points early on was the magic figure. Once we had an eleven point lead, it meant the other side had to score three times to beat us and we could conserve our resources. There was no sense in scoring 40 points in the first round, and losing through tiredness in the final.

There was nearly a disaster for me in the first round against Ebbw Vale. I had rehearsed a loop move with Gordon Britton. Bob Prosser would miss me out with a long pass and Gordon would take it instead. I would run around outside him and take a pass from him only for him to run around outside me again and take another pass to score.

Now Gordon was the most unclassical of players. He looked ungainly and his attacking brilliance was of an unorthodox variety. He is the one centre I knew who could cut inside, run straight into a bunch of forwards and come out the other side with the ball before they'd recovered from the shock. Anyone else would have been hammered, but not Gordon.

Bob missed me out. Gordon took the pass. He passed the ball to me as I looped outside and I was off. As I got to the thickest part of the defence, I made to pass to Gordon outside on my right. I looked, I blinked, Gordon was not there. I didn't know what to do and before I could make up my mind, I was crashtackled by Arthur Lewis of Ebbw Vale and now of Wales. I went flying and the ball went loose. I got up off the floor, gingerly feeling my shoulder and to my astonishment, there was Gordon trotting in under the posts. He had been on my inside all the time and collected the loose ball to score. We won 13-0.

In the second round, we beat Llanelli 12-3, and in the semi-final, we met Cardiff. They had a fast clever side who lay up on us all the time but we exploited this by tactical kicking over their heads and collecting the loose ball to score. We won that 11-0 and had an easier victory than it sounds over Newbridge in the final by 9-8 with Brian Price scoring two tries.

That made the Newport record in the sevens since 1954 read Played 44 Won 40 Lost 4. For 434, Against 176. It was quite a tradition.

I did not play in the 1966 sevens as Brian, Stuart and I were in New Zealand with the Lions but Newport lost to Cardiff in the final 23-20 in extra time.

That Cardiff victory gave an added edge to the 1967 sevens. Not that it needed it as far as we were concerned. We were separated from Cardiff in the draw and the only way we could meet was in the final. They had Tony Williams, one of the famous Cardiff Williams brothers in the B.J. role and two real fliers in Maurice Richards and Gerald Davies. In their half of the draw they were convincing, beating Newbridge 14-8, Glamorgan Wanderers 18-3 and Ebbw Vale 18-5.

We met Maesteg in the first round. Eventually we ran out winners 18-6 but it was harder than it sounds. Newport were favourites, Maesteg were the underdogs and the psychological pressure was very much on us. It was a factor that I as captain and B.J. who had returned to the club in a coaching capacity, had to deal with. This I enjoyed, master and former pupil working in harness as joint masters.

Many of the smaller clubs suspected that Newport's continual successes in the Snelling sevens was based on weeks of special sevens training sessions. This is completely untrue. We normally had one, or at the most two. The secret, as much as anything else, was that experienced sevens players could discuss a move or a tactic and understand it well enough to execute it in a match without elaborate preparations. It was the thinking which counted.

We upset some people before the tournament opened by picking Keith Jarrett, the hero of the England match, only as a reserve. We reasoned that Keith's place kicking would be less of an asset in a sevens game, and that his relatively slow recovery might cost us possession. If the ball goes loose at a tackle, falling on it quickly to regain possession is at a premium. In fact a scramble in the corner still cost us a Maesteg score and they were temporarily the Arms Park heroes until both John Anthony and I had long runs to score tries.

As we came off the field to rest for the next round, B.J. rushed on, draping us in coats and wraps to keep us warm like so many sweating racehorses. I was the major focus of his attention because I had torn an Achilles tendon in the England v Wales match and, again, the wiser course would have been to withdraw from the sevens. I spent the wait between the semi-final and the final with my leg immersed in a bucket of iced water to reduce the swelling while Keith came out of the stand and stood by in case I did not make the final. I had to put up with some vintage B.J. language for my stupidity in taking goal kicks in one of the rounds and exaggerating the effect of the injury. For my part, I had never been on a losing Newport sevens side, and this wasn't going to be the first. I was determined to make the final. I was equally determined that Newport would win.

In the second round we met a Llanelli side, with a sevens reputation based partly on the Llanelli Grammar School successes in the Public Schools sevens at Roehampton. Despite Norman Gale's place kicking, we beat them 18-5 and that took us into the semi-final against Bridgend.

Bridgend and Newport cancelled each other out with some ferocious tackling early on but we refused to be put out of our stride, and two good tries gave us the opportunity to win easily 15-5. I had now scored four tries myself although I had aggravated my injury when turning awkwardly in the Llanelli game.

We were determined to beat Cardiff. I can remember clearly Maurice Richards speeding off when the sides were level and realising that somehow, leg trouble or not, I had to catch him. Urgency must have added a yard to my speed for I overhauled him ten yards from the line and saved the situation. It had a psychological effect on Cardiff too and they began to tire badly. They still scored fifteen points to our twenty-one, but we scored a good last try to clinch the game. I got the ball from the scrum, Gordon Britton dummied with me and as I raced up to Gerald Davies I had only to pass to John Anthony to give him a clear fifty yard run to the line. Cardiff were too tired to chase and he walked the last twenty yards.

In addition to the pleasure of collecting another winner's tankard, I was presented with a cup as the outstanding player of the tournament. Not only was this gratifying as a player but I had a keen personal reason for coveting the new trophy. It had been donated by Mrs Everson in memory of her late husband Bill Everson who had been so kind to me in my early days at Newport. It was exactly the right note on which to say goodbye to the Snelling sevens for the last time. It was not, however, my last union sevens tournament—that came in the following September and turned out to be the most eventful of my career.

# 13. I TAKE THE MONEY

At the beginning of the 1967-8 season, I was invited to tour Ireland with the Wolfhounds. Des O'Brien ran this Irish equivalent of the Barbarians and asked Brian Price and I to appear. By any standards this was an attractive tour with Irish hospitality ensuring that the social aspects of the tour matched the character of the rugby. We happily accepted.

Meanwhile, the Newport secretary had received a letter from the Davenport Rugby Union Club in Manchester inviting Newport to enter a side for their sevens tournament which was to be held on a Sunday for a mentally handicapped children's charity. The Welsh nonconformist conscience still looming large in such matters, no Welsh club could officially play on a Sunday, however, the Newport committee came up with an ingenious alternative. Newport could not appear either on the field or in the programme so the decision was taken to send seven players under the captain's name. We were to be the David Watkins VII who would play in red shirts, not Newport's black and amber.

The confusion over dates meant that Brian and I were unavailable and the occurrence of a David Watkins VII without David Watkins, looked likely. That it did not turn out like that stems from my obsession with sevens. If there is going to be a sevens tournament somehow I have got to play in it. After two games in Ireland, I went to work on Ben with some sevens propaganda. Brian knew as well as the next man when he was on a good trip, so he was reluctant to leave, but I nagged some more. He finally agreed, probably more to please me than himself. We approached the Wolfhounds committee and asked if we could be relieved of the next match down in the south so that we could get to Manchester.

They were magnificently unselfish about it. It was already late on the Saturday night and the logistics of the operation were formidable. Timetables were consulted, our return air tickets to Cardiff were transferred for a flight to Liverpool and telephone calls went off in all directions. We had a few hours sleep and were then taken to the airport for a flight to Liverpool.

At Davenport, the local officials swung into action and their side of the operation was just as frenzied and, indeed, just as efficient. We stepped on to the tarmac at Liverpool, we were rushed through customs as if we were visiting royalty, and bundled into the back of a 3.8 Jaguar before we could draw breath.

Flasks of coffee and chicken in a basket appeared as if by magic, and our driver headed for Manchester as if he were driving in a Grand Prix. We squealed to a halt outside the Davenport ground, barely twenty minutes before the kick-off in our first round match against Wilmslow.

Being Newport in all but name, we were naturally on our mettle and wanting to win. We heard on arrival from the rest of the team that there was an added needle. The other star guests were Harlequins, holders of the Middlesex Sevens title. They were old rivals anyway but Colin Payne, their England second row forward had tried a bit of B.J. style gamesmanship. He stated loudly that he couldn't understand all the fuss and bother of getting a Newport team in the programme whatever they were called. They were not going to win and it was a waste of time and money their coming all the way from Wales to be beaten.

We beat Wilmslow, and wins over Chester and Broughton Park took us into the final. Opponents? Harlequins, of course! In the final itself, we really cut loose. We were told by people in the clubhouse that it was the finest display of sevens they had ever seen. The result 20-0 to Newport was very gratifying in the circumstances.

We mingled in the clubhouse afterwards with other players and spectators where the manner of our victory was the main topic of conversation. One old acquaintance who I had not seen since his union days, was John Mantle, the hero of the South African Test and now a prominent rugby league player. After we had swopped reminiscences and talked about the tournament, he asked me if I had ever considered turning professional. I explained that I had not really considered it, that it would take a lot to persuade me to give up rugby union, and that anyway I could not believe that anyone would be seriously interested in me at this late stage in my career.

I did not tell John that in common with most young talented players in Wales, I had been approached in the past. Scouts had discreetly enquired my intentions after games but I had been adamant that I was not interested. They can be persistent, and there were times when representatives had called at the house to talk to me and to talk to my parents to get them to persuade me. It had all been to no avail. One club brought a famous player with them to try to persuade me and even put £5,000 in a tidy green pile in the middle of the dining room table like a fly in front of a hungry trout. Rugby union remained too big an attraction for me to seriously consider a move to the north and gradually the offers petered out as by 1966, they lost interest in the face of my apathy.

I could hardly believe that any club would be likely

to chase David Watkins now. I forgot all about the conversation with John Mantle and went home. I had been working for a finance company for five months, enjoying it greatly, and was beginning to settle in to the new job. At the office next day I had a surprise telephone call from John. He told me that the Chairman of the Salford Rugby League Club, a Mr. Snape, had been watching my play at Manchester the previous day and had been sufficiently impressed to say that he would offer me £8,000 to play for them. If I thought there was a possibility of my accepting would I ring Mr. Snape at a Manchester telephone number.

As I have explained, this was the first offer for a number of years and I suppose I must have given it some thought but the figure of £8,000 seemed so unrealistic that I half dismissed it. I decided no one would seriously offer me so much money and I did not ring.

A few days later, I was in the office and again the telephone rang. This time it was Mr. Snape himself. He said that he would much prefer to talk to me personally than discuss the matter on the telephone but certainly he would confirm an offer of £8,000 in writing. Sure enough, in the post next day was an official offer of £8,000. I told him on the telephone that the 1967 All Blacks were on their way and that I was determined to do my utmost to captain Wales against them. After I put the receiver down and after the confirmation by letter, I began to think more seriously about it.

I could see that Salford were certainly keen to secure my services. They were prepared to offer £8,000 just like that. I would have been less than human if it had not crossed my mind that they might offer even more, if I showed interest myself. I loved rugby union, all my friends were involved in the game and I had a new job which I liked, how could I put all that at risk? And yet...

and yet. What about the future? Could I afford to give away the chance of financial security just for a few more seasons at an amateur game? I had to find out more about it at least.

As confidentially as possible, I secured the services of a solicitor to advise me and I began to discuss the matter with the people closest to me. I discussed it with Jane, who had become increasingly important in my life. I talked to Gwynne Walters who had been instrumental in helping me to get my new job and I talked it over with my parents. Most of them said firmly that I must make up my own mind but my father was really upset. His life had more and more revolved around watching his son play rugby. He will still tell you with tears in his eyes that when I went North, the joy for him was taken out of rugby union. He has kept a cabinet with all my caps, jerseys and souvenirs in it which he refuses to part with, and although he knows I took the right decision, he still feels it keenly. Can you wonder that I was in a turmoil about the decision?

I fretted, worried and veered from one opinion to another and back, minute by minute. Salford had not been idle either. A contract came through the post offering me £11,000 to sign and £1,000 per annum for five years. It was a record offer to an amateur and the colossal sum staggered me. I had been seen at a Newport v Cross Keys match at Pandy Park talking to Bob Prosser, who Salford were trying to get transferred to set the old Watkins and Prosser partnership in action again. To add to the pressures, press speculation on my future status hit the headlines. With this new and surely final offer, I had to make up my mind.

I travelled up to Birmingham to my firm's head office and discussed it with them. I told them I had been offered a very large sum to turn professional. If I accepted, would

I still have a future with the company? If they had said no, I think I would have resisted even this added temptation, but they made a marvellous gesture. Understanding how much so large a sum must mean to me, they said that if I did decide to sign, they would transfer me to a branch in Manchester. So, if I did sign, it meant that I would not be going to a strange place and looking for a new job, all at the same time.

With all sorts of doubts in my mind, I decided I would be stupid not to sign. To secure my future had to be my first consideration and I would face the other problems as they came. I agreed to go to Tewkesbury to meet the Salford representatives and sign the contract. On a Wednesday evening I travelled with Newport to Abertillery to play my last game of rugby union, knowing that the next day the solicitor and I would be going to Tewkesbury.

I enjoyed the Abertillery game despite the load on my mind but what I did not enjoy was lying in bed that night wondering if I had done the right thing. Problems build up in the small hours of the morning to gigantic proportions. Would the Welsh officials and followers hold it against me? Would they think I was throwing all their kindness and loyalty back in their faces? Would they think me a traitor to the game that we all loved? I really was a soul in torment.

I was called next morning and I did not want to get up, I wanted to close my eyes and pretend it had all been a dream. It took me ninety minutes to summon up enough courage to get up and dress. I met the solicitor and we left for Tewkesbury, and I still did not know if I could bring myself to sign.

It was October 19th, 1967, the date is still implanted in my memory. We got to the rendezvous, the Royal Hop Pole Hotel, at lunchtime. We were greeted in the car park by Mr. Snape the Chairman, the Club Secretary and the Coach and invited in to lunch. I could no more have eaten than flown at that stage, I was so tense. I had to sit at a table in the dining room with an empty plate in front of me while the others ate their lunch.

Throughout the meal, the three of them, who were very cordial and helpful, gave me a potted history of the club, outlines of future plans, stories of great players who had signed for them, and answered every question I put to them. We adjourned to the lounge and the conversation continued. After an hour, the contract was put in front of me. I took out my pen then sheer panic set in. 'I'm sorry,' I said, 'I can't sign. Can I have a coffee?' Five times over the next two hours they gave me the contract, and five times I gave it back. They were very understanding and patient although I was reducing the proceedings to something out of a French farce. I had more coffee, some tea, a cold drink and an unbroken sweat. The sixth time, my solicitor glanced over the contract again and I signed. I was a professional. I had signed for a record fee to play a game I had never seen.

I rang Jane, who went around to my parents to tell them that I had signed. To fulfil past promises, I rang J. B. G. Thomas, of the *Western Mail* and Brian Wall of the *Football Echo* for them to have the story. Still full of doubts, I went home. I knew the prejudice previous changes of code had evoked in Wales, and I was apprehensive of being on the receiving end.

Perhaps because everyone realised how difficult such an offer was to refuse, they were kindness itself. My post next morning was full of letters from well-wishers and friends without a hostile one among them. Tony Lewis of Glamorgan was even good enough to write and welcome me to the professional ranks. I decided to write two letters myself—one to Newport and one to the Welsh Rugby

Union. In both I tried to tell them how grateful I was for what they and rugby had done for me, and in my heart how reluctant I was to leave. The spontaneous feeling of gratitude still remains with me.

When I went to Newport to see Martin Webber to whom I was leaving the Newport captaincy, complete strangers stopped me in the street and shook my hand to wish me every success at Salford. My doubts began to dissolve, particularly when Bill Clement of the Welsh Rugby Union replied to my letter with a letter which I shall treasure for life.

WELSH RUGBY UNION

Royal London House,
28/31 St. Mary Street,
Cardiff.

Dear David,

I acknowledge your letter of the 24th October, the contents of which are much appreciated by me, and will I am sure be equally appreciated by the Selection Committee and others. While I must confess to the feeling of acute disappointment with your decision to turn Professional, I would hasten to wish you well in your new sphere. You may be assured that your new career will be followed with great interest.

May I now express to you my appreciation and thanks for your tremendous contribution to Welsh Rugby in recent years. You have been a great credit to Wales both on and off the field, and our loss is the Professional game's gain.

Your energy, enthusiasm and dedication to Wales will be sorely missed on our rugby fields, but as in the past I am sure that in due time we will again be able to fill the serious gap in our playing ranks as a result of your departure.

Once again many thanks for your letter, and my sincere and lasting wishes for your future success, both in Rugby League Football and in life itself.

Yours very sincerely,
W. H. Clement
*Secretary. W.R.U.*

By a coincidence, Jane's 21st birthday party was taking place at the Tredegar and Rhymney Golf Club on the Thursday night and I still owe her an apology for the way it turned into an unofficial send-off for me. Players and friends like Dennis Perrott, Bill Morris, Brian Price and B.J. came in and out, photographers' flashes went off and only the family realised that it was really her party, not mine.

Celebrations and congratulations in Wales were one thing. I had taken the money which was nice for me. The very next night, Salford wanted me for a Friday game against Oldham. How was I going to show I could justify the gigantic fee? It was rather like jumping off Newport Bridge to see if I could swim.

# 14. GONE NORTH . . . A TERM OF TRIAL

I travelled up to Manchester by car with Jane on the Friday ready for the game in the evening. Mr. Snape met up with us at the Knutsford service station on the M.6 and led me to a hotel near Salford. Until I found a place to live, Salford put me up at the hotel for four months and did everything which could have been done to make me feel at home.

The Snape family took Jane off sight-seeing and shopping, and I was left at the hotel to rest up for the evening's game. At the hotel, there was also a hurried rehearsal while Jackie Brennan, the captain and the club coach Griff Jenkins, combined to show me how to play the ball after a tackle. Learning to get up and heel the ball back on a hotel carpet may sound a bit makeshift but it was very necessary. Racking my brains, I couldn't even remember seeing rugby league on television so you can guess how much I knew about it.

The evening was on me very quickly. I had a lie down but my brain remained obstinately active and I was glad when Mr. Snape returned to take me to the ground.

He is a remarkable man. He is as near a multi-millionaire as makes no difference, with a variety of interests, hotels and restaurants included. He played full back for Broughton Park at rugby union but succeeded his father as Chairman of Salford R.L.F.C. when his father died. Since then, he has built up Salford as a social club second to none, and no man could do more for his hobby. In my opinion, his policy of buying star names is justifiable in every way and he deserves success for the way he has tried to inject life into a sport which, it seems to me, television has brought into decline.

Like Everton in soccer, we have been accused of buying success. This attitude I cannot understand. Surely, the crowds wish to see good players and good teams. By buying good players you are attracting the crowds and the money they bring can be invested in improving the standards of the club and buying more good players. What sport has ever succeeded without personalities? I think men like Mr. Snape have done the game a great deal of good.

I found out later that he had had little sleep over the two weeks while I and Salford were in negotiation, and in the car on the way to the ground, he was as apprehensive as I was. Having paid a record fee for a player he had only seen once in sevens, he had taken the precaution of insuring me against serious injury for £10,000, but he was still nervous. So nervous in fact, he nearly sent both of us up in a puff of smoke by trying to throw his cigarette end out through the window. The window was closed and we disappeared under a shower of sparks.

At the ground itself we found extra reasons for being nervous. Not only was there a big turn out by the press and by the photographers, but the average Salford gate of 6,000 had leapt to 14,000. 14,000 people all ready I felt, to say, come on Watkins, let's see how good you are. I had some allies in the crowd in Brian Price and Peter Rees who had travelled up especially to lend moral support, but two didn't seem many out of 14,000.

In the dressing room, I was equally apprehensive. I was introduced to the rest of the team and I felt they would be less than human if they did not resent the new boy getting so much money. Peter Smethurst, one of the forwards broke the tension by saying,

'We don't care a damn how much they've paid for you. You help us to win games and you'll be putting money in all our pockets. That's what matters.'

That was good to hear, as was a Welsh accent from the corner from David Evans, a former Welsh youth player. 'All the best, Dai.' I didn't like to admit that as I put on my red jersey and saw everyone putting on shoulder pads, I began to wonder what I had let myself in for. Seeing two players, Terry Ogden and Joe Southward on crutches, one with a broken leg and one with torn ligaments, did just as little for my morale.

In the game itself, the steadying presence of Jackie Brennan proved invaluable. He told me to keep out of the way and when he felt I could usefully contribute, he brought me in. In that first season, I sometimes heard criticism that I was not doing enough but in fact, I was doing what I was told. Jackie knew a lot more about it than the critics and I am sure he was right to use me as he did.

In this first match against Oldham, as near as I could I played rugby union although I had to restrict an automatic temptation to kick for touch, and to learn not to release the ball when I was tackled. The subtleties of covering were beyond me, and I was a million light years away from dominating the game as a rugby league half-back can. I soon found out I was no Hardisty.

One thing I would plead for, is an extended period for a rugby union player to be shown patience by league colleagues and fans. I estimate it took me a full two years to rid myself of the habit of automatically releasing the ball. This is so hammered at one in union that it becomes second nature and takes a long time to unlearn. I was lucky in the tolerance and understanding I was shown but, believe me, I needed it.

The Oldham game was a false indication of the new game in many ways. After twenty minutes, I picked up a loose ball and ran seventy yards for a try. I added two more drop goals and scored seven of our points in a 12-6 win. I was chosen for the Players No. 6 award as Player of the Match, which meant an extra £6, and went home with a winner's pay packet. How much I had still to learn was lost on me, and I suppose I would have said then that union and league were basically the same. It took longer to find out that they were no more similar than baseball and cricket.

I now believe that the truly great rugby league player has to be brought up in the game. I think the difficulties would be just as great if the change were made in the opposite direction. Even a Hardisty would need two years to become a tolerable rugby union player.

Of the many things I had to learn, the first was the limited opportunities one has for a break when the opposing defence is strung out along the field. I was a marked man and I soon found it could be as important to absorb tackles and retain the ball, as it was in union to avoid them. When opponents had the ball you had to make sure they were tackled. With a financial difference between, perhaps, £8 for losing and £20 for winning, players with families might be dependent on the winning bonus and be determined to preserve it. Woe betide the careless player who lost it for them.

The new back seat role had to be learned afresh. At Newport, where I had been captain for four years, I had been at the helm. Now I had to go back to being the new boy. The rest of the Salford team nursed me admirably for the whole of the first season.

Tackling was a problem. I had always been prepared to tackle players bigger than myself at rugby union. In union this was always a possibility because an outside-half was running across the field behind the threes, and could use a tackle from the side to bring down a heavier player. When he comes at you head-on, it is considerably more difficult, my game against Workington being a classic example.

After the game had been going about ten minutes, McFarland, not the smallest of league forwards, came charging at me with the ball in his hands. I went for him and he brushed me off. On the popular side, there was a groan from the crowd—half anguished and half derisory. I got up from the turf determined not to allow it to happen again.

Ten minutes went by, and it did happen again. Paul Charlton came through with the ball, I half-tackled him and again I was brushed off. The groan this time was a bit louder.

As if fate was conspiring against me, just before half-time, another Workington forward came lumbering through and when I dived at him, walked over me as if I had not bothered. An even louder groan went up, followed by a pregnant silence. It was broken by a caustic Lancastrian voice from the terraces, audible to players and spectators alike.

'For Christ's sake, Watkins, hit 'im with your wallet!'

That, as you can guess, led to some leg pulling afterwards, with the theme developed to include my slowness being due to the weight of the money I must be carrying.

I am often asked if I am still nostalgic for rugby union, and people have suggested to me that I cannot really like playing rugby league. Perhaps some who have made the transition of codes have never adjusted to the rigorous demands of the professional game, but I should hate it to be thought that this applied to me. The finance has nothing to do with it.

Of course I can still go to see Wales at the Arms Park,

or watch a televised international, and feel an inner longing to be out in the middle in a red jersey myself. Rugby union has changed since my day, and the combination of the squad preparation and the Australian dispensation law has ensured that players are fitter, faster and more skilful. I would have loved to have had a chance to prove myself in the new style game.

That does not change my view of rugby league. I play it because I enjoy it. It is a great game and I have been lucky in playing for a great club. If I have a spare day, nothing pleases me more than to spend it watching the game I am so involved in. It is tough, and I suppose that I had only become fully adjusted by the 1969-70 season, but I am as involved with league now as much as I ever was with union. Whenever I am asked about the vigorous treatment a league player can receive, my standard reply is that I took so many hard knocks in union for fun, it's dead easy to take them for money.

Leaving union was not to say goodbye to my passion for sevens. Mr. Snape arranged at the end of my first season for Salford to be invited to enter some sevens tournaments. This must have taken some persuasion, because we were not a fashionable club, although we moved from 22nd to 9th in the league in that first season. We played first in the Halifax sevens and won it 21-18 in the final after being 18 points down. We went from there to Leeds and beat Hull Kingston Rovers 20-15 in another exciting final. In fact, we entered eight tournaments and won seven of them, including two in two days, and got to the final in the eighth, that match being the first time I had ever played in a losing sevens side in my whole career.

Salford became the Newport of rugby league sevens and we now have to contend with the majority of the crowd supporting every underdog who plays against us. The success was based on innovation, because with Bob

Prosser's assistance, we brought the Newport ideas into practice with the Salford players. Where the other sides were playing an orthodox league game up and down the middle of the field, we were experimenting with B.J. style ploys to confuse the defence. Until the other clubs had studied our ideas and produced counters, we blinded them with science.

If there is one thing rugby league could learn from union, it is the willingness to try new ideas. Because the game is so fiercely professional, there is a slight tendency to become sterile because novelty is frowned on. In fairness, union could also learn a great deal from league, particularly in backing up the man in possession. In training, there is little difference and as anyone who has sweated under B.J. and Ian McJennett will testify, it would be difficult to do much more training than we did at Newport.

One thing union could never have given me, and it took me back to the childhood ambitions of early days in Blaina, was a chance to play at Wembley. How I and Salford got there, and how we fared is worth a chapter to itself.

# 15. WEMBLEY FAILURE

Salford did not have the greatest of Cup records. Getting to the 1969 Rugby League Cup Final was their first final appearance for thirty years. In 1938, our 'Red Devils', captained by Gus Risman, had narrowly beaten Barrow 7 points to 4 but the glory of that had been soon wiped out, when only one year later, they had lost heavily at Wembley to Halifax. Back in the early days of the century, Salford had been in the final four times between 1900 and 1906, and lost the lot. It was not the most inspiring of cup traditions.

My mind was less on history, than on the desire to play at Wembley Stadium. I knew well that there were rugby league players, and some great ones at that, who had dreamed of a Final appearance and gone through careers of ten and fifteen years without ever making it. If I could get there myself in only my second season at the game, it would be quite something.

Initially at least, the draw was in our favour. We got a first round match at home against Batley, who were not the strongest league side. Just as in soccer, that is slightly misleading, because no cup match is easy and the bigger the gap in form between the sides, the less the underdogs have to lose in fighting for an upset. Fortunately for us, the form book was reliable and with Ken Gwilliam, Jackie Brennan and Ron Hill scoring tries, and Ron Hill putting over 4 place kicks, we won easily 17-2.

It was a hard, vigorous game in the early stages with some over-enthusiastic exchanges on both sides. I was on the receiving end of a series of hard tackles and occasional obstruction, but I had one of my best league games to date. Three of my attacking runs led to tries and I chased and tackled Gittins, the Batley full-back, on the line to save a try. He returned the compliment in the last few minutes, but we were over the first hurdle.

The draw for the second round brought sterner opposition in the shape of Workington Town. They had the psychological advantage of having already beaten us during the league programme but we could cancel that out by being in front of our own crowd again. The Salford crowd is warmingly partisan and we could rely on their being worth points to us at home. Our loose forward Ron Hill, a fellow Welshman who had the dubious distinction of breaking his jaw in his very first rugby league game after leaving Cardiff, was on target with three kicks, and again scored a try himself. Bill Burgess got another and we won 12-5. Ron's outstanding qualities as a tackler also contributed to our victory. One of his scything tackles injured the brilliant Workington hooker, Moss. Whether Workington ever believe it or not, this was just an accident and whatever dark rumours were started when Martin Dickens mastered the substitute easily, they are quite untrue.

Workington were not alone on the receiving end. To show for our victory, Charlie Bott had a cut eye, Mike Coulman was tackled round the throat, Alan McInnes injured his leg, and Workington's Martin was sent off for hitting Ron Hill. The bruises still seemed minor compared to the comforting knowledge that we were through.

This win gave us a quarter-final place against Widnes. Again we were drawn at home. After drawing 6,000 to the Batley game, and 14,500 to see the clash with Workington, Cup fever was really beginning to take hold at Salford, and the gates were closed three quarters of an hour before the kick-off for the game which was played on a Sunday. There was a capacity crowd of 20,000 inside and a few thousand milling around outside the ground desperate to know what was going on. We started hesitantly and Widnes were soon five points up. Our supporters were not prepared to put up with that for long, and they cheered us so much and so enthusiastically, that we began to play some of our best football. We were 12-7 up by half-time and won finally 20-7. Tries by Colin Dixon, Bill Burgess, Mike Coulman and Chris Hesketh and three goals by Ron Hill and one dropped goal by myself had taken us into the semi-final. Jackie Brennan was outstanding, selling dummies all over the place, I had another good game, and in the pack, Ron Hill, Mike Coulman and Martin Dickens covered themselves with glory.

Three days before the semi-final, we were taken along to Blackpool by Mr. Snape; the idea being to get us away from distractions and to help us to build up our concentration for the matter in hand. This is typical of the efforts he made to ensure our success. We had one hard training session when we got there, then two easy days before travelling back for the match.

The semi-final is always played on a neutral ground, and the venue chosen for the match against Warrington, the third 'W' on our list, was Wigan. We knew that we were one match away from Wembley and wondered if we could possibly play as well away from our own crowd. The Salford supporters, however, had their own ideas and when we got to Wigan, we found that forty coach-loads of supporters and innumerable private cars had preceded us. They out-numbered and out-shouted the Warrington supporters so much that it was just like playing at home. It was a hard fought game, although Warrington made many handling errors, but the star was Stuart Whitehead. Stuart, who is a close friend, came into rugby league as a youth, and was a hard, rugged second-row forward. When Salford bought Colin Dixon and Mike Coulman, he switched to the centre and it was his battering runs through the middle that brought him a try, and paved the way for two more by Paul Jackson and Billy Burgess. Jackie Brennan played on with a broken nose, and my tackling did not suffer as a result of my cracked cheek bone. We went back to the dressing room, winners by 15-8. In the dressing room, we had an emotional scene with bottles and glasses raised high. Mr. Snape was in tears. All his enthusiasm and his work seemed to have paid off. We tried to grasp the full implications of the occasion. On May 17th, in seven weeks time, Salford would be back at Wembley after an absence of thirty years.

From Wigan we were rushed back to the Salford clubhouse. We had a meal in the club restaurant, and, with the premises packed with enthusiastic members and supporters, we got up on the stage to be introduced to the fans. It was a great night, but the following day the meaning of it all began to sink in. This was the start of Salford's Wembley nerves.

The nearer May 17th got, the more apprehensive we became, and although we were contenders in the top sixteen championship play-off, losing 22-12 to Leeds, nervousness had crept into our play. We lost matches we would normally have won easily, mostly because however hard one tried, at the back of one's mind was the thought that one injury might cost one the chance of a lifetime. It was no different for Castleford, our Wembley opponents, but interest in Manchester was growing to the extent that you would be stopped in the street by complete strangers and told to make sure that the Cup was coming back to Salford. It became impossible not to think of Wembley.

If Salford was going Wembley crazy, so was Blaina. To me this was one of the most moving experiences of my life, because I was never conscious in my Welsh rugby career of a particularly personal following. Wales playing at Cardiff Arms Park would draw a capacity crowd, and the team was the important thing. Fresh news kept coming from home that coachloads and carloads would be going to Wembley to see me. It finished up with nearly 40 coaches and another 500 people in organised carloads. I sent home tickets by the hundred, and if anyone is thinking that this was little capitalist Watkins cleaning up as a ticket tout, let me tell you that I finished £15 out of pocket! When I did take the field, I was painfully aware that I was representing Blaina as well as Salford. For both their sakes, I was bitterly disappointed that I did not repay the loyalty all those people showed in coming.

We adopted the same procedure as we did for the Wigan game, but extended it to a week. We had three days together at Blackpool with diet sheets and training schedules to be adhered to, and on the Thursday we travelled direct to London. We were allowed a walk out on the hallowed turf of Wembley Stadium that day, and then we were taken to a hotel at Weybridge. There we relaxed as well as we were able, and played some golf on the hotel's own links. Friday afternoon was devoted to a team talk. Castleford players and Castleford tactics were dissected, and we were each given our personal tasks for the game. I was to look after Hardisty, and to stick to him like glue. The importance of winning was drummed in—if we could win by good football fine, but one penalty to nil would do if necessary.

I would like to stress at this point that, professionals or not, finance no longer had anything to do with it. The personal prestige of playing well for the team on this day of days, and pride in bringing honour to the club assumed much more importance as incentives. Like thirteen union players, we would have gone out and given everything without receiving a penny.

A coach came for us at Weybridge on the Saturday morning to take us to the stadium. I say a coach, but an £18,000 forty-seater limousine would be nearer the mark. With a headboard saying Salford on the front, reclining seats, a cocktail cabinet, a radio, a tape recorder, a coffee bar and a television on board, it was just another example of the way Mr. Snape did everything possible to make it a memorable occasion. We knew that his greatest ambition was to lead out the team, so we clubbed together to buy a trilby for him to carry in the traditional manner in his right hand.

Butterflies really started at the beginning of Wembley Way. We had been scanning the horizon for the famous twin towers and suddenly there they were, two hundred yards away. Even the few brave souls who had been trying to break the tension by singing, lapsed into silence. The only man who seemed unaffected was Colin Dixon, genuinely and enviably able to treat it as just another game.

The best tension-breaker came in the dressing room. We trooped in to see a table piled with good luck telegrams and hanging up at the back of the room, was a row of brand new Salford jerseys with a gleaming Salford badge on them. There were whoops of delight as we rushed to put them on. Dazzling shorts and socks, gleaming boots, even the bootlaces looked to be specially shined. Players wandered up and down admiring each other, and looking for a mirror to admire themselves.

We were ready twenty minutes before the kick-off, and we had a final run-through of tactics as the last touches of vaseline and strapping went on. Mr. Snape walked in and, after all his efforts, could have been forgiven a last minute reminder not to let him down. Not a bit of it. He made a wonderful little speech thanking us for our efforts to get this far, and said that much as he would like us to win, the most important thing was to go out and enjoy ourselves.

He was patently sincere and as soon as he had gone, Griff Jenkins the coach spoke in a rather different vein. We could forget enjoyment. He expected us to be going hard at it even if our tongues were hanging down to the floor. We owed it to the Salford supporters, to the club, and to Mr. Snape to take the cup back with us.

With his words ringing in our ears, I led the team up the tunnel to walk out behind Mr. Snape. Going out at the Arms Park is always an emotional experience but I have never heard so much noise from a crowd as that Wembley roar. All the Salford supporters were at the tunnel end, and the perspex cover around the arena holds the sound in. The volume was really frightening. It was like walking into a solid wall of sound.

The preliminaries were soon over. We were introduced to the President of the Rugby League, Lord Derby, and Prime Minister Harold Wilson. This led to some leg-pulling for Charlie Bott, our prop forward and the team's strongest socialist, it must have been all too much for him, we said, to appear at Wembley and meet his hero all in the same day.

Early on, I was robbed in a tackle, and Ron Hill kicked the penalty for 2-0 to us. Hepworth broke away from a scrum and put Howe in for an unconverted try for Castleford, 2-3. After 35 minutes, Ron Hill kicked another penalty and we were 4-3 up. This is how it still stood when we went in for the interval. We were desperately unlucky when Chris Hesketh our centre, made a forceful run through a ruck of players, but in his dive for a try, he touched the ball down on the wrong side of the line first before grounding it.

Psychologically, if that score had been allowed it could have rattled Castleford's composure at a crucial stage. Instead, they were the ones to come out and take the lead when Reilly put Hardisty in under the posts, and Redfern kicked the goal to put them 8-4 up. Ron Hill's boot brought us back to 8-6 from a penalty for a scrum infringement. We pressed hard, they pressed hard and both sides came desperately near to scoring but Hepworth crashed over in the dying seconds for an unconverted try for Castleford and they won 11-6.

Early in the game, our winger Bill Burgess was blatantly short-arm tackled and laid out cold, twenty yards away from the play. He was a crucial member of our attack and although he continued, he was too dazed to ever get into the game. I felt a sending-off would have been justified. We took a lot of punishment in the first quarter of an hour and the game was hard, rough, gruelling stuff rather than being spectacular.

Generally, we came into it in spasms but Castleford were consistently good. They won the game and probably deserved to. The one man on our side who distinguished himself was Colin Dixon. Personally, I felt utterly despondent. I felt that I had let so many people down by my own performance. I took the long long walk to the tunnel with my loser's medal in my hand and tears in my eyes.

As we lay in the bath, I let the hot water soak in to my aching limbs. We talked about the game and tried to work out how we had gone wrong. Tired as we were, I think we would have all been prepared to go out and try to replay the game more effectively but it was too late, and it took me ages to find the energy even to climb out of the bath and dress. That was almost the worst moment of the next twenty-four hours.

We went to the Royal Garden Hotel in the evening and

had a Salford dinner there for some 500, players, friends and guests. Again Mr. Snape's efforts paid off and by the end of the night, it was as happy an occasion as if we had been celebrating a victory. We began to forget the game and it was only when we caught the Manchester train next day that we began to dread going back to face the die-hard Salford supporters who we had let down so badly.

We need not have worried about hostility. There were thousands of people to greet us at the station, thousands to greet us at the museum and art gallery where the Mayor of Salford gave us a civic reception, and thousands along the route that we drove in an open double-decker bus. We could see banners with slogans like 'Sir Brian Snape', 'Dixon for Prime Minister' and 'Watkins for King' and that brought home our disappointments even more keenly. All this loyalty and what had we done in return? It was that which remained uppermost in my mind after we went from the art gallery to the Salford Club and then, late that night, dispersed to our separate homes.

Castleford, our conquerors, became a bogey team thereafter. From Wembley onwards they beat us five times running and we heard of an apocryphal story that was circulating the supporters, as always, they had the last word.

Mr. Snape was reported to be very worried about our poor record against Castleford. One day, he said to Griff Jenkins, the coach, that we had to take some action.

'Go over to Castleford, Griff, and see how they train. Bring back their methods and we'll put them into practice here. I'm going off to Majorca for a fortnight but ring me from Castleford tonight and tell me what you will need.' Griff goes off to Castleford. That evening he rings Mr. Snape.

'Well, Griff, what are they doing?'

'They've got thirteen dustbins they place on the field

in different positions, and they run in and out between them, passing the ball to each other.'

'All right, I'll leave you some money. You buy thirteen dustbins, paint them in Castleford colours, and use them in our training. I'll ring you from Majorca next week and you can tell me how things are going.'

Mr. Snape goes off to Majorca. Griff buys the dustbins. A week later, Griff's phone rings.

'Hullo, Griff, it's Mr. Snape here. How is the new training going?'

'Oh, Mr. Snape, I've got some terrible news for you.'

'What's that?'

'The dustbins are winning nine-nil!'

# 16. REFLECTIONS

In the 1969-70 season following our disappointment at Wembley, Salford did not figure in any of the major league trophies. Personally I had the consolation of having my best league season. With a combination of tries and kicks, I approached the hundred points total but the real satisfaction came from the knowledge that I had adjusted fully to the new game. Not only was I able to make up for the amateurish mistakes that I had made in my first season but as captain, I was responsible for the on-field decisions and I welcomed the responsibility. Just as in union, I think it helped me to improve my personal game by being more conscious of others' problems.

I am frequently asked, particularly by my old union friends, how long I intend to continue in the professional game. My own mind is made up, I have no intention of continuing once I lose my speed. Throughout my two careers this has probably been my major asset, and I am firmly convinced that a player's reputation can only be damaged by continuing in any game when he is past his best. The crowds, rightly or wrongly, have short memories and there is nothing sadder than seeing a man, in any sport, struggling against opponents he would once have beaten easily. As I hope I have made clear, I am enjoying my league career. I hope it will long continue and I can certainly envisage at least another three or four seasons in the game.

The enjoyment is much more of an incentive than unfulfilled ambitions. Of course I would never dream of turning down an opportunity to tour with the British rugby league team but representative honours are nowhere near as meaningful as the honour of taking the field for one's country at rugby union.

My first loyalties would always be to Salford who have done so much for me. I like to think that I will still be able to return to Wembley and walk up to the Royal Box to receive not a runners-up medal, but the Rugby League Cup to take home to our magnificently loyal supporters.

As I look back on the two careers that have taken me over ten thrilling years and all over the world, it would be churlish to close the book without my deeply felt thanks to thousands. To the people of Blaina and Wales, to the Salford supporters, to the players and officials of Newport R.F.C. and Salford R.L.F.C., to the administrators who have helped develop both codes into the great games that they are, and to my family and friends, I would like to say this—for all my personal success and, I suppose fame, I would never have progressed beyond being a part-time footballer in the Welsh valleys without their help. I truly believe that my success has been on their behalf and that they should all share in it. To me, they always will.

When I was a small boy, a day out at Lord's was spoilt for me by a famous Middlesex cricketer brushing me roughly aside when I asked politely for his autograph. I silently vowed then, that if I ever became a famous sportsman, I would never forget that it is the fans who make the stars, and that one should never forget one's obligations to them.

My ability at the rugby union game gave me everything, and I hope no one will think it arrogant or a sign of ingratitude if I use this opportunity to make a few suggestions which to my mind would improve the union game.

Make no mistake, I fully realise that rugby union as I played it until 1967, has since improved immeasurably. Players are fitter, faster and more skilful, and with the Australian touch kicking dispensation, the opportunities for the thinking footballer have increased greatly. There are still four reforms I would like to see incorporated.

First, to allow substitutes at international level and not at the other levels of the game is illogical. In league, we have the sensible rule that a substitute may temporarily replace a star player, while medical attention is given, and the star can return when, say, stitches have been put into a cut. There is then no reason why a substitute cannot come on immediately. I could not help noticing that in the 1969-70 season, Wales could easily have lost both to England and to France, when they played for a longish period in each game with fourteen men while they waited for the result of medical opinions on whether Gareth Edwards and Jim Shanklin would be fit enough to continue. The narrowness of their winning margins emphasises the point. This would be sensible at all levels of the game.

Second, I would advocate a differential penalty. Not in the sense of reducing the value of the kick but more in the nature of a free kick in soccer, differentiating between a direct and indirect free kick. For foul play, for obstruction, for deliberate offside and for similar offences, I would allow a kick at goal which, if converted would count for three points to maintain the deterrent principle. On the other hand, for an accidental or technical offence, I would give a penalty and only allow a kick to touch, adding the proviso that the side given the award would also get the throw-in. To go back to that 1969-70 Twickenham thriller which Wales eventually won 17-13, you may recall what happened when Gareth Edwards went off and there was a five minute delay before a specialist scrum-half in Ray Hopkins replaced him. During that five minutes, Dave Morris the wing forward was given the unenviable task of putting the ball into the scrum on the Welsh 25. Obviously due to his inexperience, he put it in incorrectly and was penalised for it. Bob Hiller, the England captain, just missed with the penalty but it could have cost Wales the game. Surely a kick to touch, followed by an England throw-in would have been a punishment more fitting to the crime.

My other two potential reforms would apply more to the administration of the game. Wales before the introduction of the squad system and even partly since, have long been known as the producers of more 'one-cap wonders' than most. I think this is due to the trials system. To me, trials are a farce and towards the end of my union career, I, and let us be honest, many other established players, looked for excuses or diplomatic injuries to drop out of them. An international in possession has nothing to gain and everything to lose by playing in a trial. The newcomer, on the other hand, might produce his one and only outstanding game of the season, and be capped as a result. I think that consistent club form should be the basis of selection. Sir Alf Ramsey does not have to hold trials to choose outstanding England soccer players, why should a Saturday club's fixtures be spoiled by a Welsh Rugby Union trial?

If it is felt that there must be an intermediate stage between club and country, what about building up the county system? As there are so few Welsh rugby playing counties, it should be possible, given some tactful negotiations, to get them into the English County Championship to the mutual benefit of both the Welsh and the English rugby unions in terms of crowd appeal, and of providing collateral form for international selection. With Glamorgan firmly in the County Cricket Championship for the same sort of reasons, it would not be that revolutionary. Then the dedication of county officials like Wally Talbot and Ken Gwilym might be properly rewarded.

Although I am beginning to sound like a rugby dictator, I would also change the unofficial Welsh Championship. For a title which carries so much prestige, it's a very haphazard affair. Some clubs play many more fixtures than others, some play stronger opponents and some teams in the table never play each other. I would like to see the top sixteen clubs in a first division playing each other, home and away. This would reduce the enormous load of fixtures that a club like Newport or Cardiff has to carry, to 32, and still allow them time to play friendlies against English clubs or teams such as the Barbarians according to choice. This method would produce a genuine champion club and, more important, by having a second division with a two up, two down promotion and relegation system, allow the Blainas, the Tredegars, and the Abercarns of Welsh rugby to have an opportunity to play Cardiff or Llanelli if they can hold their place. It would also bring players from the smaller clubs into the selectors' eye and kill off for once and for all the dying valleys' tradition that 'you'll have to go to Newport or Cardiff if you're ever going to get a Welsh cap'. I think this would be of considerably more value to the smaller clubs than brief lived glories in any new knock-out cup.

To conclude this book, I can reveal one unfulfilled ambition in rugby union. Since my own happy days with them, the Cwmcelyn Youth Club has closed down. If, as an ex-rugby league player, I would be permitted, I would like to return to Blaina one day in the future and try to start up a youth side there again, coaching and advising them myself and trying to return to the game some of the things it has given me. When one considers how many Welsh schoolboy internationals are lost to the game on leaving school if they do not have the academic abilities to go into colleges and universities, it would be worthwhile. If I could be there, at that crucial stage in a young player's development to assist another local boy starting out on the path I took myself, to me that would be the best possible finish to the David Watkins story.

# INDEX


Aberavon, 42, 61, 110
Abercarn, 147
Abertillery, 10, 23, 31, 122
Abertillery & Blaina Schools, 15
Albaladejo, P., 57
All Blacks 1963 tour, 32, 33-41
All Blacks 1967 tour, 97, 120
Allen, Fred, 90
Anthony, John, 32, 104, 116
Apartheid, 65-66
Arms Park, Cardiff, 11, 39, 41 43, 44, 47, 49, 67, 68, 103, 115, 130, 137, 139
Arsenal, 11
Arthur Boucher Cup, 35
Ashton, Cliff, 43
Australian dispensation, 131, 145

Barbarians, 42, 61, 147
Barrow, 133
Batley, 133, 134
Bebb, Dewi, 47, 53, 54, 55, 62, 63, 65, 70, 82, 84, 95, 103
Bedford, Tommy, 62
Bevan, Graham, 111
Blackheath, 31
Blackpool, 135, 137
Blaina, 9, 10, 13, 18, 21, 22, 23, 24, 45, 79, 99, 101, 132, 137, 144, 147
Blaina Park, 15
Boniface, A. and G., 71
Bordeaux, 22
Bott, Charlie, 134, 139
Bowcott, Harry, 73
Bradshaw, Keith, 52, 54, 56, 57, 63, 74, 75, 76
Brennan, Jackie, 126, 128, 133, 135, 136
Bresnihan, B., 75
Bridgeman, Sem, 9
Bridgend, 29, 30, 42, 52, 112, 115
Bridgend Sevens, 23
Briscoe, Kevin, 59
Bristol, 39
British Lions, 19, 42, 65
British Lions 1966 tour, 75, 77-98
  First Test v. Australia, 81-82
  Second Test v. Australia, 83-84
  First Test v. NZ, 89-90
  Second Test v. NZ, 92-93
  Third Test v. NZ, 93-94
  Fourth Test v. NZ, 94-98
Britton, Gordon, 113, 116
Brophy, N., 102

Broughton Park, 119, 126
Burgess, Bill, 134, 135, 136, 140
Burgess, D., 43, 98
Burnett, Roy, 27

Cambarabero, Guy, 103
Campbell-Lamerton, Mike, 77, 78, 79, 80, 92, 93
Canada XV, 43
Cape Town, 60
Cardiff, 30, 31, 32, 39, 42, 45, 46, 54, 56, 75, 101, 103, 111, 114, 116, 134, 147
Cardy, A., 81
Cardiff City, 11
Castleford, 136, 137, 139, 140, 141
Caulton, Ralph, 37
Charlton, Paul, 130
Cheney, Ray, 23, 38
Chester, 119
Chisholm, D. H., 97
Clarke, Don, 34, 36, 37, 40, 60
Clement, W. H., 57, 124, 125
Club Row, 9, 10, 11, 14
Coleman, David, 73
Coles, Fenton, 23
Colombes, 71, 75
Combined Glamorgan and Monmouthshire v. Fiji, 67
Cooper, Russell, 12, 13, 15, 17
Coulman, Mike, 134, 135, 136
County Championship, 146
County Cricket Championship, 146
Crauste, Michel, 50, 57, 71
Craven, Danie, 57, 58
Cresswell, Brian, 26
Cross Keys, 110, 111, 121
Cunningham, L. J., 40
Cwmbran, 43
Cwmcelyn Park, 13
Cwmcelyn Youth, 17, 18, 27, 32, 109, 147

Darrouy, C., 76
Davidge, Glyn, 26, 27, 36, 110
Davies, Beverley, 20
Davies, Evan, 17
Davies, Geoff, 26, 42
Davies, Gerald, 114, 116
Davies, Leighton, 29, 30
Davies, Stuart, 110
Davenport R.F.C., 117
Dawes, John, 55, 56, 70
Dedieu, P., 72
Derby, Lord, 139
Dick, M., 95
Dickens, Martin, 134, 135
Differential penalty, 145
Dix, Allan, 29, 30
Dixon, Colin, 135, 136, 138, 140, 141
Dourthe, C., 103
Dublin, 55, 74
Duggan, A., 102
Duprat, B., 76
Du Preez, F., 62, 63

Ebbw Vale, 16, 23, 31, 113, 114
Edwards, Gareth, 74, 100, 102, 103, 145
Engelbrecht, J., 63
England, 14, 22, 30, 43, 44, 46, 47, 48, 68, 72, 103, 105
English, Mike, 49

Evans, Colin, 23
Evans, David, 128
Evans, R. T., 24, 26, 27
Everson, Bill, 25, 35, 116
Everton, 127

Falkman Trophy, Joseph, 18
Fijian tour of Wales 1964, 67, 68
Flynn, M. K., 71
*Football Echo*, 20, 100, 123
Ford, Ian, 26, 36, 37
Ford, Trevor, 11
France, 15, 21, 43, 50, 56, 66, 71, 75, 76
Frankcom, Geoff, 69

Gachassin, J., 22, 71, 103
Gainsford, John, 60
Gale, Norman, 70
Gelli Grug Secondary Modern, 13
Gibson, Mike, 56, 75, 84, 85, 89, 94, 95, 96, 102
Glamorgan Wanderers, 114
Glanyrafon Secondary Modern, 12
Gloucester, 35
Gloucestershire, 39
Goodall, Ken, 102
Graham, John, 40
Grant, Derrick, 78, 80, 87
Gray, Ken, 87
Gwilliam, Ken, 133
Gwilym, Ken, 147

Halifax, 133
Halifax Sevens, 131
Hampton Court, 52
Hardisty, K., 128, 129, 137, 140
Harlequins, 31, 52, 118, 119
Hayward, Dai, 40, 44, 45, 46, 47, 52, 63
Hepworth, K., 139, 140
Herewini, Mac, 89, 97
Hesketh, Chris, 135, 139
Hill, Ron, 133, 134, 135, 139, 140
Hill, Rowland, 15
Hiller, Bob, 146
Hinshelwood, S., 95
Hitchens, Gerry, 11
Hodgson, Grahame, 47, 49, 53, 54, 56, 73, 102
Hopkins, Ray, 146
Hopwood, Doug, 59, 62, 63
Horrocks-Taylor, J., 53
Howe (Castleford), 139
Howells, Bryn, 14
Hughes, Brigadier, 42
Hull K.R., 131

International Board, 57, 60, 67
Ireland, 43, 48, 49, 50, 55, 56, 70, 101, 117

Jackson, Paul, 136
Jackson, Peter, 46, 47
James, Rumsey, 18
Jane, 101, 103, 123, 125, 126
Jarrett, Keith, 104, 105, 106, 107, 115
Jenkins, Griff, 126, 139, 141, 142
Jenkins, Vivian, 48, 50
Johannesburg, 62
John, Barry, 101

Jones, Benny, 23
Jones, Brian, 26, 29, 30, 31, 32, 33, 34, 35, 36, 37, 38, 55, 108, 109, 110, 111, 112, 114, 115, 118, 125, 132
Jones, Cliff, 20, 44
Jones, Ken, 54, 55, 62, 73, 74, 75, 81, 89

Keogh, F. S., 56
Kennedy, Ken, 82, 89
Kiernan, Tom, 70, 71
Kirton, Earl, 36
Knock Out Cup, 147

Lacaze, P., 76
Laidlaw, Chris, 96
Lamont, Ronnie, 78, 86, 89, 94, 95
Laughland, Ian, 54
Leeds, 131
Leicester, 28
Leonard, Ken, 23
Lewis, Alan, 19, 72, 74, 82, 96, 101, 102
Lewis, Arthur, 15, 113
Lewis, Tony, 123
Llanelli, 30, 40, 51, 55, 110, 114, 115, 116, 147
Lochore, Brian, 90
London Welsh, 12, 52, 55, 65
Love, Pat, 65
Lydney, 35

MacRae, Ian, 37, 97
Maesteg, 42, 114, 115
Mantle, John, 52, 63, 119, 120
McBride, Willie John, 78, 81, 85, 90, 95
McJennett, Ian, 33, 34, 35, 132
McFadyean, Colin, 90, 93, 94, 95, 96, 105
McFarland, 130
McInnes, Alan, 134
McLean, Terry, 86, 94
McLoughlin, Ray, 78, 95
Malan, Avril, 59
Marais, J. F. K., 63
Martin (Workington), 134
Meads, Colin, 41, 90, 93, 95, 96, 97
Meredith, Bryn, 26, 28, 33, 84, 110, 111
Michaelson, Roger, 44
Middlesex Sevens, 118
Midlands Colts XV, 22
Molloy, M., 70
Monmouthshire, 107
Monmouthshire Schools, 15
Monmouthshire Youth, 18, 19
Morgan, Bob, 40, 47
Morgan, Cliff, 11, 12, 15, 21, 27
Morgan, Haydn, 78
Morgan, Roy, 32
Morley, Jack, 31
Morris, Bill, 125
Morris, Dave, 111, 146
Morris, John, 34
Murphy, Noel, 82, 84, 88, 92, 94
Murphy, Pat, 93
Murrayfield, 48, 49, 101

Nantyglo, 11
Nathan, Waka, 34, 35, 36, 37, 38, 94, 95
Neath, 29, 30, 31, 111, 112
Newbridge, 9, 31, 104, 114
Newport County, 11

Newport R.F.C., 24, 26, 27, 28, 29, 30, 31, 32, 42, 44, 45, 51, 52, 54, 55, 79, 80, 99, 102, 104, 117, 118, 119, 121, 122, 123, 124, 129, 131, 132, 144
Newport v. All Blacks 1963, 33-39
Newport v. Australians 1966, 100
Newport in Sevens, 108-116
New Zealand, 33, 34, 65, 67, 84-98
Norris, Howard, 90, 98
North Wales, 107

Paris, 50
Pask, Alun, 40, 47, 57, 58, 60, 61, 63, 70, 72, 73, 77, 78, 87, 95
Payne, Colin, 118
Penarth, 26, 27
Perrott, Dennis, 27, 37, 125,
Perry, David, 53, 72, 73
Phillips, Dave, 61
Phillips, M. S., 47
Players No. 6 award, 129
Pontypool R.F.C., 23
Pontypool Youth, 19
Pontypridd, 23
Poole, Keith, 36
Powell, Graham, 11
Price, Brian, 26, 27, 33, 34, 35, 36, 39, 40, 61, 64, 65, 78, 88, 89, 95, 110, 111, 112, 114, 117, 118, 125, 127
Price, Terry, 68, 69, 70, 71, 72, 73, 102, 103
Prosser, Bob, 34, 35, 37, 38, 39, 51, 109, 110, 113, 121, 132
Prosser, Ray, 23
Prothero, Gary, 22, 68, 75, 78, 83, 87, 88
Public Schools Sevens, 115

Rainbow team, 14
Ramsey, Sir Alf, 146
Ranson, J., 53
Redfern (Castleford), 140
Rees, Alan, 42, 43
Rees, Peter, 29, 30, 31, 55, 56, 127
Reilly (Castleford), 140
Rhymney Valley Schools, 15
Richards, Maurice, 114, 116
Richards, T. B., 43
Risman, Gus, 133
Roberts, J., 47
Robins, John, 80
Rodney Parade, 11, 25, 27, 37, 38, 43, 46, 67, 100, 104
Rogers, Budge, 53, 72, 78
Rowlands, Clive, 35, 39, 41, 43, 44, 47, 48, 49, 50, 52, 53, 54, 56, 57, 61, 62, 70, 71, 72
Royal Garden Hotel, Kensington, 140
Royal Hop Pole Hotel, Tewkesbury, 122
Royal Hotel, Cardiff, 45
Rugby League Cup Final, 1969, 133, 139-141
Rutherford, Don, 68, 73, 82

St. Helens, Swansea, 110, 113
Salford, R.L.F.C., 120, 121, 124, 125, 126, 127, 129, 131, 132, 133, 134, 135, 136, 137, 138, 139, 141, 143, 144

Scotland, 48, 49, 54, 55, 56, 69, 97, 101
Shackleton, J. A. P., 49
Shanklin, Jim, 145
Sharp, Richard, 46, 47
Simmers, B. M., 70
Snape, Brian, 120, 123, 126, 127, 131, 135, 136, 138, 139, 141, 142
Snelling Sevens, 108-116
Somerton Park, 12
South Africa, 57, 66, 67
South Africa, Wales Tour of, 60-65
South African Jubilee Matches, 57-60, 62
South African Rugby Union, 57
Southern Counties, 33
Southward, Joe, 128
Smith, C. M., 63
Springboks, 63
Squad System, 131, 146
Steel, A. G., 97
Stradey Park, 19, 20, 21
Swansea, 39, 43, 52

Talbot, Wally, 147
Taylor, John, 65
Taylor, Bob, 72
Telfer, Jim, 90, 94
Thomas, Alan (Algie), 36, 39, 40, 100
Thomas, Alan, 61
Thomas, Brian, 40, 44, 53, 54, 69, 70
Thomas, Byron, 110, 111
Thomas, Delme, 93, 94
Thomas, J. B. G., 48, 123
Thomas, Malcolm, 11, 108
Tredegar, 42, 112, 125, 147
Tremain, Kel, 37, 38
Trials, 146
Triple Crown, 31, 56, 67, 70, 71, 74, 75
Tulle, 21, 22, 75
Turner, Jock, 74
Twickenham, 14, 52, 72, 73

Uzzell, Dick, 34, 36, 37, 38, 39, 40

Wales, 11, 14, 20, 21, 24, 30, 32, 39, 40, 43, 44, 45, 47, 50, 54, 57, 67, 71, 101, 120, 130, 144, 145, 146
  v. Australia, 101
  v. England 1963 (Cardiff), 46-48
  v. England 1964 (Twickenham), 52-54
  v. England 1965 (Cardiff), 68-70
  v. England 1966 (Twickenham), 72-73
  v. England 1967 (Cardiff), 103-106
  v. France 1963 (Colombes), 50
  v. France 1964 (Cardiff), 56-57
  v. France 1965 (Colombes), 71-72
  v. France 1966 (Cardiff), 75-76
  v. France 1967 (Colombes), 102-103
  v. Ireland 1963 (Cardiff), 49-50
  v. Ireland 1964 (Dublin), 55-56

WALES, *cont.*
v. Ireland 1965 (Cardiff), 70-71
v. Ireland 1966 (Dublin), 74-75
v. Ireland 1967 (Cardiff), 101-102
v. New Zealand 1963, 39-41
v. Scotland 1963 (Murrayfield), 48-49
v. Scotland 1964 (Cardiff), 54
v. Scotland 1965 (Murrayfield), 70
v. Scotland 1966 (Cardiff), 73-74
v. Scotland 1967 (Murrayfield), 101
v. South Africa 1964 (Durban), 62-64
Wales under 23 XV, 43
Wales XV, 67
Wall, Brian, 100, 123
Walsh, Pat, 37, 65
Walters Gwynne, 38, 121
Warrington, 135
Watkins, Billy, 25, 26, 34
Watkins, Stuart, 37, 54, 55, 56, 57, 58, 68, 70, 74, 76, 94, 105, 112, 114
Watt, B. A., 41
Weaver, D., 52
Webber, Martin, 124
Welsh Rugby Union, 67, 123
Welsh Secondary Schools, 19, 20
Welsh Trial, 11, 42, 43, 99
Welsh Unofficial Championship, 147
Welsh Youth, 19, 21, 27
Wembley, 11, 132, 133, 135, 136, 137, 138, 139, 141, 143, 144
Western Counties, 39
*Western Mail*, 20, 123
Weston, Mike, 47, 77, 82, 90
West Side Junior School, 12
Weybridge, 137, 138
Whineray, Wilson, 34, 36, 41, 59
Whitehead, Stuart, 136
Whitson, Geoff, 14, 26
Widnes, 134, 135
Wigan, 135, 136, 137
Wilcox, Ray, 11
Willcox, J. G., 53
Williams, Denzil, 44, 52, 78, 85, 88
Williams, Tony, 114
Williment, Mike, 87, 97
Wilmslow, 118, 119
Wilson, Harold, 139
Wilson, L. G., 63, 64
Wilson Stewart, 70, 80, 83, 84, 95, 97
Wolfhounds, 117, 118
Workington, 130, 134

Young, Roger, 82
Youth Selectors, 22